innovation

>> create an idea culture
>> redefine your business
>> grow your profits

Tom Gorman

BUSINESS

Adams Media
Avon, Massachusetts

Published by Adams Business, an imprint of Adams Media, an F+W Publications
Company, 57 Littlefield Street, Avon, MA 02322
www.adamsmedia.com

ISBN 10: 1-59869-154-6
ISBN 13: 978-1-59869-154-2

Printed in Canada.

J   I   H   G   F   E   D   C   B   A

Library of Congress Cataloging-in-Publication Data
Gorman, Tom.
  Innovation / Tom Gorman.
      p. cm.
  ISBN-13: 978-1-59869-154-2 (pbk.)
  ISBN-10: 1-59869-154-6 (pbk.)
  1. Creative ability in business. 2. Success in business. I. Title.
  HD53.G668 2007
  658.4'063—dc22   2007001126

This publication is designed to provide accurate and authoritative information with
regard to the subject matter covered. It is sold with the understanding that the publisher is not engaged in rendering legal, accounting, or other professional advice. If
legal advice or other expert assistance is required, the services of a competent professional person should be sought.

　　—From a *Declaration of Principles* jointly adopted by a Committee of the American
　　　　　　　　Bar Association and a Committee of Publishers and Associations

Many of the designations used by manufacturers and sellers to distinguish their product are claimed as trademarks. Where those designations appear in this book and
Adams Media was aware of a trademark claim, the designations have been printed
with initial capital letters.

This book is available at quantity discounts for bulk purchases.
For information, please call 1-800-289-0963.

contents

THE SKILLS OF INNOVATION

INNOVATION IN ACTION

iii

part 3

INNOVATION IN SPECIFIC SITUATIONS

introduction

The Engine of Endless Success

One morning several years ago, I was shuffling to work with a herd of other commuters in Grand Central Station in Manhattan. We were headed through a double door leading out to the street, but one of the doors was closed, forcing us to file slowly through the single open door. When I reached a point a couple of yards from the doorway, I heard a guy not far behind me call out, "Could some innovator please open the other door?"

A woman just ahead of me opened that door, instantly doubling the flow of commuters out to the street. The guy, of course, was being sarcastic and the woman hadn't been particularly innovative. But the incident made me think: Why hadn't someone opened the other door when the crowd clogged the exit?

There are reasonable explanations. Maybe people assumed the other door was locked. (The janitors have their little jokes, you know.) But then wouldn't someone have tried the door and found it unlocked? Perhaps people thought someone before them must have tried to open the door, so why bother trying it? Or maybe we all figured that once we got to the door, who cares? We were hitting the street, so the devil take the hindmost.

All of these are reasons for lack of innovation: assuming the worst, leaving it to someone else, and just not caring. There are other reasons why people don't engage in innovation, which you'll learn about in this book. But more important, you'll learn reasons for innovation, and how to go about this exciting, profitable activity.

What Is Innovation?

Innovation is the act of developing a new product, service, or process based upon a new idea. The root word here is *novus,* which means "new." An innovation is something new. To innovate means to come up with some new thing, not just a new idea. Ideas are wonderful; I like ideas, and I make my living working with them. However, an innovation is the physical form of the idea—a new product, service, or process that you can use to make money.

Many people have an "idea" for a product, service, business, movie, or book (trust me on that last one), but then they fail to develop the idea. Developing an idea means making it bigger, richer, clearer, more detailed, and more useful. It means putting it into a form you can show to other people and, with their help, make something of it and launch it into the world. You'll learn how to do that in this book.

Innovation goes on in every field of human endeavor. Innovators are problem solvers, and innovation is problem solving. Everywhere you look there are problems to solve—some long-standing, some new. In a market economy, you can do a lot of good and make a lot of money by solving problems. Of course, in a market economy these "problems" may include the a lack of long-distance golf balls, exotic resorts, and affordable sports cars.

Who's an Innovator?

The word "innovator" may remind you of guys wearing white short-sleeved shirts, bow ties, and plastic pocket protectors. Or perhaps you think of dynamic entrepreneurs like Steve Jobs, founder of Apple, Next, and Pixar; Steven Spielberg, moviemaker and a founder of DreamWorks; and Richard Branson, the fellow who runs all those Virgin companies when he's not bungee-jumping or ballooning around the world. However, anyone with a solution to a problem can become an innovator.

In the business world—the world I know best—most innovations come from individuals, teams, and departments. Innovators include:

- *Entrepreneurs, who get ideas for products and services and then pull together the resources needed to bring them to market.*

- *Marketers and advertisers, who find or create new needs and news ways to grab our attention and purchasing power.*

- *Inventors, who see problems they can solve with their imaginations and the materials at hand or, if necessary, materials they can make. This group covers everyone from your uncle who's trying to make ice cubes in the shape of martini glasses to laboratory scientists working on cures for dreaded diseases.*

- *Corporate research and development (R & D) departments, where people work with a company's resources and technologies to create new products and services to keep current customers and win new ones.*

If you work in any of these areas, or want to, you've got to be innovating all the time. Even if you don't innovate for a living, you'll make a better living and find life more fulfilling if you take an innovative approach to whatever you do. Every organization in every industry—financial services, health care, manufacturing, entertainment, education, fashion, retail, travel and hospitality, government, and the arts—needs innovators and rewards them well.

The Engine of the Economy

Innovation is the engine of the world's economy because there is no end to the problems in this world, and there never will be. Every business, every organization of any kind, exists to solve a problem. That means that every business and organization, and every person, has an opportunity for constant renewal by developing new solutions and new sources of growth.

Every product and service, from the highest of high tech to the lowest of low tech, solves a problem. Earphones solve the problem of noise pollution (for the wearers and for those around them). Peanut butter, jelly, and bread solve the problem of hunger at lunchtime. Health clubs solve the problem of obesity. Automobiles solve the problem of getting around without the need for train or airline schedules.

Another way of saying "problem" is "need." Every business fills a need. We need portable music, tasty sandwiches, toned abs, and personal transportation. Innovation is the process of identifying and developing solutions to problems and creating new ways to meet needs. Every day at work, each of us plays some role in the process of solving problems and meeting needs.

This book shows you how to contribute to that process. I believe that we all can sharpen our ability to identify problems and develop solutions. We all can do far more to meet the needs of our customers and coworkers. This book reflects that belief, and aims to help you develop solutions to those problems, fill those needs, and reap the rewards.

THE SKILLS OF INNOVATION

part 1

" WHAT WE HAVE BEFORE US ARE SOME **BREATHTAKING OPPORTUNITIES** DISGUISED AS INSOLUBLE PROBLEMS. "

—John W. Gardner
(social activist)

Innovation = Problem Solving

Let's start with a look at three innovations and the companies that helped make them what they are today: personal computers and Apple; overnight delivery and Federal Express; and lifestyle marketing and Ralph Lauren. These three phenomena embody key trends in innovation. In their way, each one also solved a problem, and every innovation solves a problem.

> ## in•no•va•tion
> 1. a new product, service, process, or approach to a problem
> 2. a new way of thinking about something
> 3. the act of innovating, as in "Innovation occurs in every culture"

Personal Computers and Apple

The personal computer (PC or microcomputer), which is now as common as the telephone or television, started kicking around in basic forms in the mid-1970s. It took the PC a while to find its market, which it did in the late 1980s. In the 1990s, the World Wide Web exploded, and personal computers became indispensable.

Before the PC, beginning in the 1950s, businesses used mainframe computers, mostly IBMs. The problem? They were big, expensive, and only experts could operate them. The solution was to make computers smaller and easier to use. In the 1960s, Digital Equipment Corporation (DEC) launched the minicomputer, which put mainframe power into a smaller unit. But DEC minicomputers still couldn't fit on a desk, and you still needed experts to run them. In the late 1970s, Apple and several other companies put mainframe computing power into desktop units. Shortly thereafter, thanks to icon-driven, point-and-click technology, Apple made computers easy to use.

Here's what's interesting to me: IBM, which owned the mainframe market, didn't develop the minicomputer—DEC did. And DEC, which based its business on making computers smaller, didn't develop and popularize the microcomputer—Apple did.

Sounds simple, doesn't it? Take what you sell, make it smaller and easier to use, and keep doing that. Yet as you'll see, many companies develop something new, then fail to repeat that success. In this book, we'll look at why that is, and what you can do about it.

> I don't design clothes, I design dreams.
>
> —Ralph Lauren (designer and entrepreneur)

Overnight Delivery and Federal Express

A *New Yorker* cartoon (it's always a *New Yorker* cartoon) shows a businessman pitching an idea to Santa Claus. Santa is saying, "Let me get this straight: You're going to fly all the toys to Memphis, switch the toys around to the right airplanes, and then deliver them to the right children?"

That's the idea behind Federal Express, which founded the overnight delivery business as we know it in the early 1970s. Before FedEx, people hired couriers for overnight delivery of documents and packages to distant points. Those couriers required cab fare, air fare, and a fee for having to eat airline food. The problem was how to make overnight delivery cheaper and easier. The solution required a method of transferring thousands of letters and packages among hundreds of cities overnight. You can't just fly all the parcels directly from origin to destination.

The solution was to bring all the parcels to one central point, sort them there, then fly them to their destinations. At first, the notion of sending a package from San Francisco to Memphis and from Memphis to Seattle instead of moving it directly from San Francisco to Seattle seemed weird to some people. But it works.

Lifestyle Marketing and Ralph Lauren

Lifestyle marketing goes back a long way: Even in the 1950s, certain cars, such as the Cadillac and Corvette, and magazines, including *Town and Country* and *Playboy*, appealed to people's desire for a prestigious, independent, or cool lifestyle. Yet prestigious, independent, cool lifestyles must be getting scarce, because lifestyle marketing is everywhere. Give a good portion of the credit (or blame) to Ralph Lauren.

Ralph Lauren was truly innovative when he first wrapped his clothing around a lifestyle some thirty years ago. His Polo brand was the first to use multipage, thematic ads, and the world he portrayed was as rarified as Hefner's. Essentially, Ralph Lauren took Brooks Brothers's image and cranked it up. He placed his white, blond, blue-eyed, square-jawed models on yachts and golf courses and in wood-paneled rooms bedecked with hunting prints. Brooks Brothers had taken that lifestyle for granted because their customers generally were upper-middle-class WASPs in Manhattan. Ralph Lauren, born Ralph Lifschitz to immigrant parents in the Bronx, showed everyone outside the

life•style mar•ket•ing

1. advertising that appeals mainly to the customer's emotional need for status, success, adventure, affection, and security
2. advertising that invites consumers to identify with the models or celebrities who use the product and downplays the actual product

so-called American aristocracy—all the Irish, Italian, Jewish, Polish, German, Hispanic, and Asian Americans with upwardly mobile aspirations—that they could be part of it, or at least look the part. In a multitude of ways, everyone from Martha Stewart to Sean Combs has lifted pages from this master's playbook, and he's still going strong.

Nobody Is Immune

If lifestyle marketing seems silly to you, I salute your sense of identity. But never believe you're immune to the emotional appeal of lifestyle marketing, which targets even the rebels among us. For instance, the VW Beetle has always been marketed to people who don't need a car to announce their importance. You're funky, independent, and secure—and your Beetle broadcasts that fact.

What problem did Ralph Lauren solve? The problem of how to sell more high-quality merchandise at higher prices to a larger market. Who among us doesn't want to do that?

Themes and Variations

You'll find the following themes in the cases above and in other recent innovations. Please keep them in mind as you think about innovation:

- *Technology drives innovation*

- *Innovations spread quickly*

- *Scramble competitors (whom you'll meet later in this chapter) complicate things*

- *Marketing always matters*

Technology Drives Innovation

Don't limit your definition of technology to computers and electronics. Technology is as versatile as our imaginations, and many innovations are driven by developments other than those in information technology.

Technologies such as ergonomics, adhesives, synthetic fibers, polymers, pigments, and injection molding have transformed the simple sneaker into a psychedelic array of athletic shoes. The bar-code technology that speeds you through supermarket checkout also sorts thousands of parcels per hour at FedEx. The fiber-optic cable that brings us no-longer-free television programs enables doctors to perform non-invasive surgery. The laser technology that patrolmen use to detect speeders on the highways also plays the CDs on the sound systems in our cars.

Innovations Spread Quickly

As you've surely heard, the pace of change is now faster than ever. This is as true in innovation as it is in other areas of life. Problems that used to slow the adoption of innovations, such as poor design, have been solved, while improved marketing and distribution bring products to market faster.

Developing nations adopt the newest technologies, not old ones. They don't use the telegraph, then the telephone, then the cell phone. They're going right to the cell phone. The whole world is ditching typewriters and buying PCs. China and India use the same technologies that more industrialized nations use.

A truly improved product becomes the new global standard. When a new solution exists, everyone wants its convenience and cost advantages. Companies therefore make and export their most recent generations of products, not the earlier ones. This doesn't deny the fact that health care, dental care, and nutrition remain poor in many areas of the world. It is only to say that where people can afford a solution, they use the best one available.

Scramble Competition Complicates Things

F. Michael Hruby, author of *TechnoLeverage*, coined the term "scramble competition" to describe today's business landscape. A scramble competitor is usually armed

Take Action

To see how to make money from technology as it's broadly defined, see TechnoLeverage *by F. Michael Hruby (Amacom Books, 1999).*

The solution to a problem often comes when you apply the right technology to whatever it is you'd like to do.

with a new technology or tactic and uses it to change the game. Apple did it with the Macintosh, FedEx did it with overnight delivery, and Ralph Lauren did it with Polo. The effect on established companies, such as IBM and DEC, UPS and the USPS, and Brooks Brothers, can be unsettling.

Scramble competitors come out of nowhere. Steve Jobs and Bill Gates weren't seasoned executives from established computer companies. Jobs was a journalist, and Gates was a Harvard dropout. They were guys who had strong ideas and a passion for bringing them into reality.

What Hruby calls "contest competition" is dying. The Big Three U.S. automakers— General Motors, Ford, and Chrysler— employed contest competition. That's usually a battle for market share between a few major companies in a mature industry. Contest competition feels safe and predictable to established companies, which find scramble competition disorienting. If you work for a contest competitor, beware of scramble competitors.

Wherever you work, try to adopt the methods of a scramble competitor. I'll be telling you more about them, but the basics are to identify a need, problem, or market that is not being addressed by contest competitors. Then you apply a new solution—which often involves technology—to the need, problem, or market; work with the most innovative customers; start small and stay under large companies' radars; and provide superior products and services.

Marketing Always Matters

Sometimes the innovation isn't actually a new product, but a new way of marketing and selling a product. Innovative marketing can amount to true innovation, especially given that buying and using new products has become a form of self-expression.

Branding plays a major role in this, which is why it has become the subject of intense study. Branding involves creating and communicating strong images that capture and convey to the customer certain product characteristics and emotions. Again, the product characteristics extend beyond the product

SCRAMBLE COMPETITORS

- Come from "nowhere"

- Apply technology to problems

- Target unmet customer needs

- Change the playing field

itself, and the emotions tap our psychological needs. FedEx confers importance and urgency upon thousands of trivial documents. Ralph Lauren sells status, not clothing.

A customer makes a statement when he chooses a brand. Apple positions itself as the cool alternative to corporate Microsoft. Harley-Davidson sells tradition; Kawasaki sells speed. Wal-Mart evokes value; Ikea evokes design. Budweiser means you're one of the guys; Glenlivet means you're one of the sophisticated guys. Mercedes gives you prestige; BMW gives you performance. Many of us choose products for what they say about us rather than for their utility.

Marketing, and especially advertising, are being transformed by the World Wide Web, and the fact that people are bombarded by messages. Most companies are using more new-media marketing methods.

I mention all of this because a lot of creative resources go into innovative marketing. In fact, even if you have a terrifically innovative product, you are going to need terrifically innovative marketing to get attention and sell it. More on this later.

The first sentence in the excellent book *Creativity in Business* is, "One of the main problems in U.S. business today is that there are too many ideas, not too few." Given the statistics on both new products and new product failures, that seems true. But maybe it's a case of too few *good* ideas? If so, why would that be? Why do companies develop bad ideas? Why do so many new products fail to meet their revenue and profit targets?

Here are some reasons:

○ *Technology for technology's sake. Some companies develop a product or feature just because they can. This happens when engineers or techies say, "Wouldn't it be cool if we _____?" without asking customers if they want it. They create features (say, in software) that nobody needs.*

○ *Solutions in search of problems. Why are there tiny windshield wipers for the headlights on some cars? Help me out here. Were water droplets or snowflakes really cutting the effectiveness of headlamps? Were customers really saying, "We can put a man on the moon, but we can't make little wipers for headlights?"*

○ *Poor user interface. Here I am using the term "user interface" in the broadest sense, to include bottles with hard-to-remove caps, power tools with hard-to-reach switches, and anything that comes with a manual that has twenty pages of fine print titled "Getting Started." This happens when companies don't do a good job of designing the product and testing it with real users.*

Take Action
Take a look at Creativity in Business, *by Michael Ray and Rochelle Myers (Doubleday, 1986). Based on a Stanford University course, it offers unusual approaches to business problems.*

○ Ignoring production realities. The realities of production include the cost of the plant and equipment, materials and labor, packaging and storage, and shipping and installation. You'll often hear the phrase "time to market," which means the time it takes a company to develop a new product and actually get it out to customers. The more flexible a company's production systems—and those of its suppliers—the faster the company can get new products developed and released.

○ Forgetting about marketing and sales. Most companies have stopped designing products and throwing them over the wall to the salespeople. That doesn't mean, though, that all companies have stopped doing so, nor does it mean that they fully consider the tasks that marketing and salespeople face.

Marketing and sales must be considered at the outset of any innovation effort or, better yet, drive the effort. Product developers often overlook distribution challenges. How much will it cost to ship and hold in inventory? Can wholesalers and retailers make money on the item? Will they stock the item? How entrenched is the competition, and how can you dislodge them?

Taking an innovative approach to situations means locating the problem and its cause, and then identifying and implementing a solution.

Are there innovative solutions to problems like these? Yes!

Innovation Basics
In general, people innovate most productively when they:

1. Try to improve life for the customer. Customers buy things that solve their problems or make doing the things they want or need to do easier, more enjoyable, or more profitable. Examine the customer's entire situation as it relates to your product. What are they really trying to accomplish? How does your product help or hinder them?

2. Try to deliver a complete solution. In the early days of the PC, hardware manufacturers gave relatively little guidance regarding monitors, printers, and other so-called peripherals. They also left customers to load the software into the systems. It took several years for the major manufacturers to start selling full systems with the software installed.

3. Never say, "If we make it, they will buy," which is the marketer's version of, "If you build it, they will come" from the movie *Field of Dreams*. Beware of the phrase, "We'll have to educate the market." Sometimes, customers do

- Identify the problem

- Gather information

- Develop alternative solutions

- Implement the best solution

need to be educated about a truly new product, but it's far easier to sell them something they know they need as soon as they see it.

4. Consider production and sales challenges right from the start. We'll look at ways of doing this in Chapter 6, where you'll learn to screen and evaluate ideas. No matter how great your idea for a product or service, if it costs you more to make it, sell it, and deliver it than you can charge for it, you don't have a viable idea.

5. Avoid putting good resources into a bad idea. When you realize that, for whatever reasons, a product or service isn't going to work, stop developing it. This may strike you as common sense, but in some companies politics, rather than common sense, drives decisions. Believing in an idea is one thing. Pushing for something that customers won't buy and that you can't sell is another.

Many companies have developed a keen awareness of the need to innovate and of the problems involved. The solution usually hinges on innovative ways of managing innovation. At other times, it comes down to diligent management of the product development process, which you'll learn about in Chapter 3. This is product development as it's done in major companies. It is not, however, a recipe. A lot of skill, imagination, and judgment always goes into innovation, and that's what makes it one of the most exciting and challenging pastimes in any industry.

> An inventor is simply a fellow who doesn't take his education too seriously.
>
> —**Charles F. Kettering**
> **(engineer and inventor)**

Let's turn to some basic things you need to know about innovations and new products, and the ways in which people respond to them.

“ INNOVATIONS **NEVER** HAPPEN AS PLANNED. ”

—Gifford Pinchot
(forester and
conservationist)

People and the Products They Love

To develop successful innovations, you need to know how people respond to new products and services. Not everyone likes new things, and some people cling to whatever they're used to for as long as they can. As a result, products go through life cycles that affect everything from sales tactics to rates of innovation.

An aging product line is one of the surest signs that a company's growth will slow down.

These are not theories, but proven guidelines for understanding people and products. With that understanding you can target the right customers and always know how your product is doing. To that end, this chapter focuses on how people respond to new products, and how that affects the products themselves.

pro•duct life cy•cle

1. the time the product is on the market, from launch to discontinuation
2. the four phases of introduction, growth, maturity, and decline

Adopt a Product

Everyone's different. Some people can't wait to get their hands on the latest thing, and others want to hang on to old things forever. In the early 1960s, communications professor and theorist Everett M. Rogers developed the innovation adoption curve (or technology adoption curve, or product adoption curve). This curve, depicted in Figure 2-1, categorizes people into five groups.

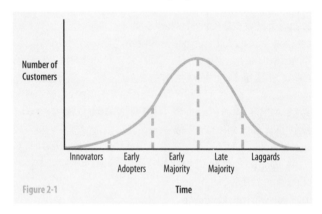

| Innovators | Early Adopters | Early Majority | Late Majority | Laggards |

Figure 2-1   **Time**

The adoption curve categorizes people vis-à-vis a specific product, service, or technology. It's not as if you are universally an Innovator, an Early Adopter, and so on. Rather you are an Innovator, an Early Adopter, and so on with regard to a *specific* product or service.

The horizontal axis depicts the time it takes for adoption to occur. It may take the

Laggards six months to adopt a product (a TV show like *American Idol*) or ten years (e-mail). The curve just says that the Innovators will use the product first, then the Early Adopters, then the Early Majority, then the Late Majority, and finally the Laggards.

The curve isn't saying that everyone will eventually use the product. For instance, not everyone will own a cell phone. However, this will be the sequence in which those who do adopt them will do so. If you sell to organizations, the curve still applies because some companies adopt new technologies faster than others.

KINDS OF CUSTOMERS

- *Innovators*
- *Early Adopters*
- *Early Majority*
- *Late Majority*
- *Laggards*

Who Are These People?

Rogers characterized the five groups under his curve as follows:

- ***Innovators*** *(2.5 percent of the market) are adventurous, even risk-takers.*

○ *Early Adopters* (13.5 percent) have the respect of other groups and are opinion leaders; they'll try new things, but carefully.

○ *Early Majority* (34 percent) are deliberate in their moves, but want to be ahead of the average person or organization.

○ *Late Majority* (34 percent) are skeptics; they wait until the product is proven.

○ *Laggards* (16 percent) value tradition and resist change.

Take Action

Check out Diffusion of Innovations, *by Everett M. Rogers (Free Press), now in its fifth edition and loaded with interesting examples.*

The adoption curve operates on several safe assumptions. First, most people won't try something until someone else has tried it. Second, people vary in their willingness to try new products. Third, it takes time for people to learn about a new product, whether through marketing efforts, word of mouth, or exposure to the product. Fourth, some people will derive more value from a new technology than others. For example, people with long commutes will derive more value from hybrid cars than those with short commutes.

Also, an individual doesn't adopt every product in the same way. Some people who can't wait for the newest kitchen appliance drive cars that can be charitably described as antiques. Some people who lease a new car every two years rarely visit their kitchens.

Have You Heard of the Herd?

The technology adoption curve bears out the idea that people operate on a herd mentality. First a tiny percentage of people try a new product. Then some other forward-thinking people see the first ones using it, and give it a try. That creates enough of an example for the majority of people to come along. Finally, there are those who lag behind the herd, either to set themselves apart or because they just can't keep up.

Do Niche Markets Expand?

A niche market differs from a mass market. In a sense, it includes only enthusiasts, who resemble Innovators and Early Adopters. Niche market products don't usually fit the adoption curve, and to sell to those customers you have to live in their world. For instance, consider the market for speed metal music. It's not as if once 2.5 percent of listeners latch on to speed metal, those Early Adopters are going to jump in (and I fear the Laggards will never really get with it).

niche mar•ket

1. an inherently small market for a specialty product
2. a specialized market for a more widely distributed product, such as the home office market for photocopiers

Yet niche markets can expand unexpectedly. Organic food, gourmet cookware, and cosmetic surgery are all now pursuing the mass market.

Niche markets show the wisdom of thinking small. You can become the source, or one of a very few sources, of a product for enthusiasts.

It's Alive!

While the technology adoption curve describes customers, the product life cycle explains the product. The product life cycle traces a product's arc from launch to growth to maturity and decline. If you understand product life cycles, you'll always know where your product is headed.

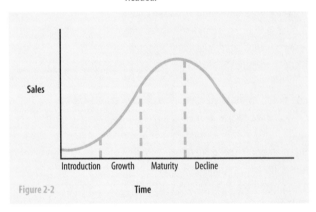

Figure 2-2

Like all of us, products go through a generally predictable life cycle. Figure 2-2 shows the classic product life-cycle curve.

Here are the key points about the product life cycle:

○ *As with the product adoption curve, the horizontal axis is time. Over some period of months or years, most prod-*

ucts will go through these phases.
I say "most" because fad products
have very short maturity phases.

○ You can gauge the phase a product is
in by its sales figures. During introduction, sales will be slow or will progress
in fits and starts. The growth phase
kicks in when sales rise at an increasing rate. Maturity comes when growth
levels off and sales remain stable.
Decline begins when sales decrease.

○ The length of each phase varies by
product. A specific product may have
a steeper or softer growth trajectory, a
longer or shorter maturity, or a sharper
or gentler decline. The introduction
period also varies. Some products,
such as the TV show Seinfeld, take a
while to find their markets; others, like
American Idol, win instant acceptance.

○ You have to change your marketing
and sales tactics as a product goes
through its life cycle. The technology
adoption curve implies that you're
selling to different customers at different phases. In a way, you're also
selling a different product.

○ Product life cycles have sped
up over the past twenty
years. The telephone took
about seventy-five years to
reach maturity, while VCRs
took about fifteen years.
Shorter life cycles are driven
by rapid technology development, increasing global

Fads are the kiss of death.
When the fad goes away,
you go with it.

—**Conway Twitty**
(country music singer)

25

competition, and greater information about needs and problems.

The Match Game

The product adoption curve and the product life cycle give you two views of the same situation—people buying products. As you would expect, the Innovators, Early Adopters, and some of the Early Majority buy the product during its introduction and growth phases; some of the Early Majority and the Late Majority purchase it during its maturity. The Laggards jump in when the product is in decline.

This has implications for you as an innovator because the product and customers change, and change demands innovation. You're never selling the same product, because something cannot remain new for long. Cell phones are not the product they were ten, five, or even two years ago. The people now buying their first PDAs (personal digital assistants) are obviously not the people who bought their first PDAs three years ago. The marketing and sales challenges change.

To manage a product throughout its life cycle, you first have to know where it is and where it's headed, then adjust your tactics accordingly. To determine the phase of a product, examine its sales figures as explained earlier in this chapter.

Introduce with Impact

During the introduction phase, sales may be sluggish or spotty. You're trying to win acceptance for the product or service among the Innovators and then the Early Adopters. Innovators can be hard to reach, but once you have their attention, they will listen to your pitch. They are knowledgeable, and they must see you as equally knowledgeable.

You use a personal approach with Innovators and even Early Adopters because there are few of them relative to the size of the market. Also, because you'll be charging a relatively high price—once you can start charging, that is—it often pays to have some Innovators use your product free and then buy it if they like it (or just keep it). Remember that Early Adopters watch the Innovators, so even if you win some Innovators by giving away the product, they are worth winning.

You have to get your product to the Innovators, even if you give it away to some of them, just so they'll know about it and talk it up to other customers.

For any innovation, introduction is the make-or-break phase of the life cycle. Tactics and tools include product placement, endorsements, buzz and viral marketing, free samples, and guarantees. I'll discuss these tools in Chapter 8, which covers product launches.

Manage Growth Aggressively

In the growth phase, the challenge shifts from marketing the product or service to making and delivering it. In his book *Inside the Tornado*, author and consultant Geoffrey Moore advises a company experiencing the rapid growth of a "market tornado" to "just ship." The goal is to fill orders, to just get the product out the door.

That's all well and good if you are in a growth tornado. What if you're seeing a slow growth phase—sales growth has picked up, but you're not in a tornado?

In that case, you must keep the Innovators and Early Adopters happy. If they become dissatisfied, you are in trouble, because, as you've already learned, the Early Majority watches those market leaders. A market tornado may allow you to "just ship," but slower growth demands that you

Critics Have Influence

During introduction, reviewers and critics can make or break some products. For instance, automotive writers loved the Mazda Miata, one of the first retro roadsters, and helped it win acceptance. They hated the Pontiac Fiero and the revived Ford Thunderbird, and both of those cars died. Did the critics "kill" those cars? Probably not, but car fans read car columns and magazines; after poor reviews, few would be eager to test-drive those cars.

keep customers happy. When someone has a problem, fix it. Unless a competitor is already on your tail, slow down production or delivery to make sure that you get things right. Getting things wrong can generate negative word of mouth, which can kill your product.

Aside from that, the challenge in the growth phase shifts to leveraging your early success. Spread the word. Make sure the Early Majority knows that Early Adopters are happily using the product. Endorsements can be invaluable at this stage. Early Adopters want assurances that the product is dependable, and that you'll fix any problems that do pop up. They don't want to be guinea pigs.

> I think that our fundamental belief is that for us growth is a way of life and we have to grow at all times.
>
> —**Mukesh Ambani (Chairman, Reliance Industries Ltd., India)**

Milk Maturity

A mature product has found its market and no longer has to seek acceptance. Instead, it has to battle competitors. One common weapon is price cutting, which can reduce the product's profitability. Fortunately, there are other ways for a mature product to compete with immature upstarts or even aging opponents. Here are four tactics:

○ *Position the product as the original and best. Marketing that plays on the* product's heritage, the company's experience, and customers' brand loyalty has helped many a mature product milk its maturity stage.

○ Develop product enhancements, such as new features and updated versions, or product line extensions, or both. This strategy must work for food and consumer packaged goods outfits, because they have made product proliferation the cornerstone of their marketing plans.

○ Watch out for new technologies, products, and services that could supersede your product. For instance, the U.S. Post Office didn't see FedEx coming. On the other hand, Standard Register, a business forms company, did see print on demand, desktop printing, and electronic forms on the horizon. That company used its expertise in printing and routing to stay relevant.

○ Copy or incorporate the best attributes of new competitive products—or buy them out. Major soft drink companies, including Coca-Cola and Pepsi, saw the threat in the rising tide of bottled water and energy drinks. Coke now sells Dasani water and Rockstar energy drinks, and Pepsi sells Aquafina and AMP.

Take Action

To learn how an aging brand revived itself, read More than a Motorcycle: The Leadership Journey at Harley-Davidson *by Rich Teerlink and Lee Ozley (Harvard Business School Press, 2000).*

Deal with Decline

It helps to see decline as a natural stage in the product life cycle. Some business people don't, which leads them to blame it on clueless salespeople or disloyal customers. If you remain calm, you can do several things to preserve profits as the product rides into the sunset, and maybe even reverse the decline:

TO DEAL WITH DECLINE

- Sell the heritage

- Use new packaging and distribution

- Hold or increase prices, if possible

- Minimize investment in the product

- Emphasize the product's heritage and nostalgia value. Harley-Davidson revived itself as an ironclad American brand after decades in the doldrums.

- Look to new technologies for new packaging and distribution methods. Imagine how happy the rock stars and record executives of the 1960s were when they realized their vinyl records were being rereleased as compact disks.

- Consider holding prices steady, or even increasing them. Brand loyalty can run deep. Even with European luxury cars sparkling in their showrooms, some American motorists just won't drive anything but a Cadillac or a Lincoln. Even with cigarettes linked to lung disease and banned in nearly every public place, many people keep puffing away. People who really want certain products care relatively little about what they cost.

- Don't overinvest in a declining brand. One of the great things about the product adoption curve is that you know what lies ahead for your product, even if you don't know when. Once a product starts declining, however, consider your next action.

> **BUSINESS HAS TWO—AND ONLY TWO—BASIC FUNCTIONS: MARKETING AND INNOVATION.**

—Peter Drucker
(author and
management
consultant)

Innovation the Corporate Way

3

Many of us picture innovators as garage-based entrepreneurs or as lone inventors toiling away in their basement workshops. Although those images sometimes fit, many of today's innovations come from team efforts at major companies.

Yet, the image of the lone inventor or entrepreneur leads some of us to believe that large companies can't innovate. Some can't, but many can. Outfits such as 3M, Apple, Hewlett-Packard, Motorola, and big consumer packaged-goods companies including Procter and Gamble, have a very good record of new product development. Whatever their faults, large corporations have the resources and discipline to develop processes that generally produce the desired results.

> **new pro•duct de•vel•op•ment**
>
> 1. the act of conceiving, designing, testing, building, and launching new products and services for customers
> 2. the department or function in an organization responsible for developing new products

In this chapter, then, we look at product development as practiced in many large companies. Yes, as noted in Chapter 1, product development efforts often fail. But they also often succeed, sometimes brilliantly. A product failure doesn't always mean the company screwed up; it often just reflects the difficulty of developing successful products in tough markets. While major corporations may not always be hotbeds of innovation, most are run by intelligent, dedicated men and women. Also, as you'll see in Chapter 10, many companies insulate product development teams from the bureaucracy that undermines innovation. So it's worth knowing how they go about it.

Let's See What Develops

New product development works best when you have a clearly defined problem and a few potential solutions. The approach can start from either a marketing viewpoint or an engineering viewpoint, but usually combines people and principles from both disciplines.

Here's what I mean: A marketing viewpoint starts with customers' needs and desires. What do customers want in terms of features, performance, and price? What do they value? What do they value enough to pay for? What do they like about our competitors' products? Should we copy or improve on those features?

Products and Services

In most of this book, but especially in this chapter, when I say "products" I also mean "services." So the product development process explained in this chapter also applies to developing services, which is mainly where I've used it. It's common for service companies, particularly in banking, insurance, and other financial services, to talk about their "products" even though they are actually services.

Engineering—the department that designs products—tends to assume that the customer's needs are known. Often, they *are* known—thanks to market research. Also, engineering can safely assume that customers want certain things. Run-flat tires are a great example. If you ask customers, "Would you want tires that you could drive on safely even after they went flat?" no one's going to say, "No, I like changing flats, especially in the rain." Sometimes, though, engineers develop a product or feature just because they can. ("Little windshield wipers for headlamps would be *sooo* cool.")

In most companies, marketing and engineering work much more closely than they once did. Until about twenty-five years ago,

KEYS TO PRODUCT DEVELOPMENT

- Know the customer

- Solve customer's problems

- Use cross-functional teams

- Follow an orderly process

35

Take Action
For a good overview of marketing research in general, visit www.quickmba.com

engineers would design a product, then throw it over the wall to production. Production would make the product, then throw it over the wall to marketing. Marketing would come up with advertising and promotions and throw them over the wall—with the product—to the salespeople. As a result, salespeople would sometimes come back saying, "We can't sell this."

Most companies use cross-functional product development teams to scale the walls between departments. A cross-functional team includes someone from each department involved with a product. That way someone from production can say, "Hold on, we need to make this product with cheaper materials or we'll lose money on it." Or a salesperson can say, "Wait, we're not really set up to reach the target customers for this product."

The product development process makes innovation orderly. It's a set of logical steps that lead to a product or product enhancement (a new feature for an existing product) that you can profitably sell. A step-by-step approach helps you know where you are and whether it's worth it to go to the next step. That's a key point. You need to know when to cut your losses. An orderly development process provides feedback to help you make the product more salable or, if that's impossible, to abandon the idea and move on to a better one.

Think of product development as orderly innovation. It's a process for channeling creative efforts into marketable results.

Six Steps to Success

New product development generally occurs in six steps:

1. Idea generation
2. Concept testing
3. Prototype design
4. Product testing
5. Market testing
6. Product launch

Let's take a look at each step.

Step 1: Got Ideas?

Product ideas come from various sources, with your customers or target customers among the best. They are the people who have the problems you're trying to solve. So, to get good product ideas, listen to your customers, especially to their complaints. (I know—it's not easy.)

Customer satisfaction surveys and focus groups will tell you what customers think. Satisfaction surveys ask what they like and dislike about your products and the way you do business. You can use mail or Web-based questionnaires, or telephone or personal interviews, to learn about customers' problems, needs, and opinions. Focus groups gather six to twelve customers together to discuss their needs and wants or to gauge their response to product concepts. A focus group leader asks the questions and keeps things on track. Members of the marketing team watch from behind a one-way glass, from where the session is videotaped for later analysis and viewing.

However you go about it, be sure to ask questions that may lead to good ideas for new products and services.

Be on the Lookout

Keep an eye on your competitors through your sales force, in the press, at trade shows, and on the Web. If they get a better idea, maybe you can improve on it. Also, monitor government regulation and social trends. Home-equity lines of credit exploded after Congress disallowed the tax-deductibility of interest on credit-card debt. Social trends generate so many new products that I examine that subject in Chapter 5.

Instead of asking only about product features that customers would like, ask more basic questions that will spark their thinking—and yours:

○ *How do you use the product? What do you use it for?*

- How often do you use it? Do you use it more often or less often than you did a year ago? Three years ago?

- What would you like the product to do that it cannot do now?

- How does the product fit your lifestyle or (for a business) your operation? Is it easy to use?

- What problems do you have with the product? What makes it hard to use?

- What do you like least about the product? What do you like most about the product?

- If you could change one thing about the product or service, what would that be?

Also, if your business has salespeople, be sure to occasionally ask them for product ideas. They talk to customers (and prospects) every day and face the challenge of selling the products. Good questions to ask them include:

- What are the biggest barriers to a sale?

- How could you sell more?

- What do customers ask for? What do they tell you that they would like to see the product do?

- *What holes do you see in our current product line?*

- *What competitive products do our customers like best, and why?*

Step 2: Test the Concept

A product idea may emerge as an actual product concept, when you "see" the product right away. Or, you may need to develop the idea into a product concept.

For example, take the idea of placing microchip object-sensors around a vehicle to warn the driver of nearby people and objects. That's an idea, but it's not a product *concept*. Is the product a warning system? A safety system? An accident avoidance system? Should it sound an alarm or flash a warning light on the dashboard, or both? Should the chips be hidden in the trim? Would people be motivated to buy the system for itself, or only if they got a break on their car insurance? You need to answer those questions, at least provisionally, so that you can present the concept to some customers and see how they respond.

In a concept test, you gather potential customers' reactions to the product concept. It's a form of market research among likely customers for the product. Concept testing can be done in either of two ways:

> I like to tell people that all of our products and business will go through three phases. There's vision, patience, and execution.
>
> —**Steve Ballmer**
> **(CEO, Microsoft)**

- *You can describe the product concept in detail and ask the respondents a structured set of questions about it. (By structured, I mean that you pose the same questions in the same way to each respondent.)*

- *You can show respondents a prototype of the product, then pose structured questions. A prototype, particularly a working prototype, brings the product to life for potential customers. However, don't try to "sell" the concept. True research gives respondents an objective picture of the product or service and gauges their honest responses.*

Much of what passes for research in business (and politics) is not real research. Instead, people gather support for a decision that's already been made or a viewpoint that management already holds. Real research starts with no preconceived outcome. It presents the subject to respondents objectively and seeks true opinions. To get objective research, many companies use external market research consultants and insist that they not be identified to the survey respondents.

The prototype needed for a concept test varies with the industry and product. In magazine or newsletter publishing, a mockup of the cover and page design can bring the idea to life. For software, screen shots can do the job without any actual

flow chart

1. a diagram that depicts the sequence of tasks and decisions in a process performed by people, machines, or software
2. flow-chart: to create such a diagram

programming. For appliances, tools, or vehicles, you can use clay models, computer simulations, or working models. For a service, you can flow-chart the sequence of events in the delivery of the service, such as the phone call from the customer, the steps in fulfillment, the billing sequence, and so on.

Of course, the more elaborate the prototype, the more expensive it will be to produce. The choice depends on your budget and what the respondent needs to see to understand the concept. For instance, the microchip object-sensor could be concept-tested by describing the idea, by demonstrating it with models, by conducting a test drive in a car fitted with a simple prototype of the system, with computer modeling, or even with bumper cars. One approach would be to use the cheapest way of conveying the concept, while reserving the option of using a more expensive one in a later test.

Whether you simply explain the product, show a drawing, or provide a prototype, typical questions to ask respondents in a concept test would include these:

○ *Do you understand the product and what it would do?*

- *How do you currently accomplish what this product would do?*

- *What would you change about the product?*

- *Would this product solve a large, costly problem?*

- *How frequently might you use this product?*

- *What products do you see as competitive with this?*

While concept testing is almost always worthwhile, you can sometimes omit this step, such as when the idea represents a small change to an existing product and you know it has worked for a competitor.

For example, if you're adding a new flavor to a line of beverages or an inexpensive feature to an appliance, you may be able to go right to designing and testing the product. Don't spend time and resources testing concepts you know you're going to develop anyway.

Step 3: Design and Build the Product or Service

There's a story of a meeting among the managers of a U.S. photocopier company. Their engineers took apart a Japanese competitor's product and laid out all its parts on a table. The engineers and managers inspected the results and said, "What an unsophisticated machine. Look how few parts it has." Then the production manager said, "Yes, but we could produce that one a lot faster and a lot cheaper."

The point is that you have to think about how costly and time-consuming your innovation will be to produce—and to sell, deliver, install, and maintain. In general, the simpler something is, the better. The fewer moving parts, the better. The easier it is to package, ship, stock, and display, the better.

Key considerations for products include assembly time, equipment and labor, floor space and warehousing costs, strength and cost of materials, shipping and maintenance, breakage, freshness, and so on.

Key considerations for services include the number of "touches" (interactions) required by you and the customer (some "touches" may be automated), skills of the people needed to deliver the service, information systems requirements, sequence of events, measures of satisfaction, and complexity of special service when a customer requires it.

This is when designers, engineers, materials specialists, programmers, and other technicians bring the product to life. But the entire development team must ensure that any barriers to making, selling, or using the product are identified and addressed at the design stage, including costs for the customer.

Depending on the product or service, you don't have to have the entire production and delivery system in place. You need only to have enough of it in place to make and deliver the products or services needed to run the product test.

> There is no such thing as a failed experiment, only experiments with unexpected outcomes.
>
> **—Buckminster Fuller (inventor and social philosopher)**

Step 4: The Product Test

Once the product or service actually exists, but before it goes into production, a product test will tell you how well it works for customers. A taste test for a new cake mix, beverage, or gum will be pretty straightforward. Software, medical instruments, and aircraft involve complex product testing.

Marketing and engineering should jointly conduct the product test. For some products, companies combine the product test and the market test (the next step). If possible, keep the two steps separate because they address two separate issues. The product test addresses product issues: Does the product or service work as we anticipated? Is it properly designed? Can customers use it? How do they use it? Do they like it? Does it fit their lifestyle or business? What would they change about it? Meanwhile, as you'll see in the next section, the market test addresses marketing issues.

In many businesses, product tests involve recruiting beta-site customers who agree to

be•ta-site

1. a customer uses a product before it's released and reports his or her experiences to the company developing it

2. beta site: a customer participating in a beta test. (Beta, the second letter of the Greek alphabet, here means the next party to test the product after the developers.)

field-test the product and provide feedback. Beta-site participants are not motivated just by the joy of helping a company develop a product. They are usually Innovators or Early Adopters who want something that might give them a competitive edge, which means you may have to give them discounts or free usage for a while beyond the beta test.

During a product test, you find and remove the bugs and kinks in the product before launching it to paying customers. Participants know it's a test, so they forgive the bugs and kinks. Be sure, however, to identify not just problems with the product, but their causes as well. These might originate in the product's:

- *Design:* Are there design flaws that affect construction, durability, performance, or user friendliness?

- *Instructions:* Do users quickly see how to use the product, or are huge amounts of training involved?

- *Performance:* Does the product perform as we intended and as the user expected?

- *Usage:* Do people use the product in unexpected ways or in ways that we should accommodate?

○ **Quality and durability:** Was the product built correctly? Is it free of defects? How much maintenance is required? Does the appearance or performance of the product erode over time?

The answers to such questions help you improve the product before putting it into production and releasing it to the entire market.

Step 5: Market Testing

A market test gathers information about customers as *buyers* of the product and allows you to gauge buying behavior by offering the product to a sample of the larger market. The market test gives you a fix on your pricing; on your marketing, sales, and distribution process; and on how much and how often customers will buy. You can also experiment with different prices to see which one maximizes sales and profits.

At this point, you will have ideas about how to advertise the product. A market test will tell you whether those ideas work, and what adjustments to consider. You want to get reactions to your product literature and sales methods, which can be in close-to-final form without being written in stone.

Be sure to include tough prospects in the market test. If you go only to Innovators, Early Adopters, or customers who already love your products, you may skew the results. True, Innovators and Early Adopters will be the first to use the product. But if you intend

YOU MUST TEST

○ Design

○ Instructions

○ Performance

○ Usage

○ Quality and durability

to reach the masses, include some Early and Late Majority types. You can identify them by how long they took to purchase products you've introduced in the past.

There are several ways to test prices. One good method is to start high and then slide the price downward during the market test to see if lower prices boost sales. Another way is to try different prices in different customer samples, which can be subsets of your customer base divided by geography, industry, or size. Avoid launching a new product at too low a price. A low price may produce more sales, but if it's too low, you're leaving profits on the table. Also, it's much harder to raise prices than to lower them.

At each step of the product development process, you have a chance to change the product, target a different market, or drop the idea.

Step 6: Launch the Product

You can launch, or roll out, a product in various ways. You can do it gradually, starting with several cities or states, or you can do it regionally or even nationally. Launching a new product represents a topic unto itself, so I devote a good portion of Chapter 8 to it.

For now, here are a few ways to heighten the chances of a successful product launch:

○ *Be sure to perform the first five steps of the product development process properly. You can't expect a success-*

Take Action

For additional information on product development, visit www.beginnersguide .com *and search for "entrepreneurship" and "product development."*

ful product launch after slapdash product testing and market testing.

○ *You might try a make-a-little, sell-a-little approach. That is, instead of a broad-based product launch, work with a few (paying) customers and build up to larger production quantities, improving the product as you go along. This won't work for mass-produced items, but it works well with specialty products such as consulting services, designer furniture, and couture clothing.*

○ *Prepare your salespeople and anyone else in your distribution system. Innovative products can confuse salespeople and retailers. If they don't understand the product, they won't sell it. Give them enough sales support—training, demonstrations, and service—to get the rollout rolling. Also, use the standard marketing tools that make sense, including free samples, discount coupons, and promotional displays.*

> If you pretest your product with consumers, and pretest your advertising, you will do well in the marketplace.
>
> **—David Ogilvy**
> **(advertising executive)**

Finally, expect the unexpected. No matter how disciplined your development process and how well prepared you are, things will go wrong. Try to view them as part of the process, but be sure your customers and distributors don't suffer. If they do, you will sour them on the product.

Shoulder the blame for any glitches, fix the ones you can fix, compensate people for the ones you can't fix, and forge ahead.

" I DON'T CARE IF THIS PICTURE **DOESN'T MAKE A DIME,** AS LONG AS EVERY MAN, WOMAN AND CHILD IN THE COUNTRY COMES TO SEE IT. **"**

—Sam Goldwyn
(film producer)

The Hollywood Model

4

In Chapter 3, we examined the way many large companies develop products, such as consumer packaged goods and business equipment. But what about less tangible, less traditional products, such as films and entertainment? How are they developed? Also, what if you don't work for a company with product development resources? How can you produce an innovation when you're on your own?

The answer is what I call the Hollywood model.

A Model for a New World

An alternative name for the Hollywood model could be the production company model because independent film producers and television producers use the model. A producer conceives or buys an idea, develops a script, recruits and hires the

pro•du•cer

1. someone who finances and organizes the resources to make a film, stage a play, or create radio or TV programs
2. someone in any line of work, such as sales, who gets results

actors and crew, plans and schedules the project, raises the financing, arranges distribution, and manages the marketing and release.

The Hollywood model of innovation applies not just to films, television shows, videos, and Web sites, but also to areas of event planning, retail merchandising, and advertising. The producer's skill set also comes in handy for managers at the many companies who hire certain talent only when needed. Companies have always hired freelance copywriters, artists, and designers, but now they outsource many former staff jobs in order to keep staffs small and payrolls low. This means that managers in many companies must now act like producers. They need innovative ways to find, reward, and collaborate with talented people who aren't on staff.

> They don't call it "show art."
> They call it "show business.
>
> **—Anonymous**

If you're an independent innovator, you need to know how to find and develop ideas and how to bring together a team to bring your ideas into reality. If you want to build a business, the production model can work until you can afford full-timers. Then again, you might want to avoid the expense and hassle of a full-time staff forever. You can either build a business or just bring innovations to market with the Hollywood model.

Why Look to Hollywood?

You may think that looking to Hollywood for models of innovation is akin to hunting for sponges in the desert. It's true that movies based on blood, blowups, gross-out humor, and old TV shows can't be described as innovative. Nevertheless, the United States stands first in the global film industry. At the box office, American movies lead in every country where they're shown, and for technical excellence they have no peers. Moviegoers worldwide clearly enjoy American movies, which are among the most dependable U.S. exports. Also:

- *Moviemakers are customer-focused.*

- *It's an essentially innovative business.*

- *Moviemaking is problem solving. Aside from solving the problem of what to do on dates, the industry repeatedly overcomes new problems.*

As noted above, much of U.S. business resembles the movie business in various ways.

The range of movies mimics that of business itself and goes from tiny Web-based films that resemble (or are) home businesses, to medium-budget efforts that are like mid-size companies, to $100-million-plus blockbusters that resemble the major corporations that release them.

EVERY MOVIE

- *Starts with an idea*

- *Combines diverse talents*

- *Must be financed somehow*

- *Needs its own marketing program*

- *Stands or falls on its own profit-ability*

The movie business is definitely worth examining for methods of conceiving, developing, and distributing innovations.

First, I'll give you an overview of the Hollywood model. Then, we'll examine each phase more closely.

Sell It Again, Sam

One idea from the movie business that has found expression in general business is that of selling the same or similar content in various ways. Movies are released in theaters, television, cable, DVDs, and foreign markets. Similarly, RainToday.com was spun off from the Wellesley Hills Group, a firm that helps professional services firms market themselves. RainToday.com has grown by "repurposing" the parent company's and its own (and others') content in newsletters, reports, seminars, and on the Web.

Four Steps and a Model

The Hollywood model is composed of four steps:

○ Development

○ Preproduction

○ Production

○ Postproduction and launch

Take Action
If you're interested in learning about actual independent film production, check out the book Independent Feature Film Production, *by Gregory Goodell (St. Martin's Press, 1998).*

Development

Development is the initial phase in which the producer, director, or screenwriter gets an idea and writes or commissions a script.

The idea may come from a novel, article, news story, or an earlier movie. A producer or director with an idea gets a screenwriter to write the script. Screenwriters write scripts based on their own ideas, or those of producers or directors. Wherever the idea comes from, development results in a project for which the basic elements needed to make the movie are in place—the script, key talent, budget, and vision of the finished film.

pro•ject

1. a series of tasks performed to create a desired result
2. a complex task that demands skills of various people working on deadline
3. the result of the task itself

Preproduction

Preproduction includes everything the creative team must do before shooting begins. This entails hiring the actors and crew, raising the financing, scouting locations, and deciding on the look of the movie.

Production

Production encompasses everything necessary to shoot the movie. Here, leadership of the project tends to pass from the producer to the director (although these may be the same person, or two people working together on all phases).

The director must draw forth people's best efforts, usually in a spirit of collaboration.

Postproduction and Launch

Postproduction assembles the product and launches it into a world that may or may not be ready for it. Marketing and publicity pave the way, but the fact remains that the movie business is as unpredictable as any other, if not more so. Successes and failures are public, and given commitments to release the movie in other channels, it's hard to completely pull a failure off the market.

> Cinema is a kind of pan-art. It can use, incorporate, engulf virtually any other art: the novel, poetry, painting, sculpture, dance, music, architecture.
>
> —Susan Sontag (author)

Like most creative endeavors, a movie is the result of thousands of decisions that add up to the whole. As in traditional product development, the success of each step depends on the solid execution of the previous one. Now let's look at each step more closely.

Development: Conceiving and Crafting Ideas

Why do so many people get an idea, then do nothing with it? I'm talking about good ideas for Web sites, books, films, products, services, and businesses, and about people who know they have a good idea. I believe many of them just don't know the next step to take, which is to develop the idea. I briefly discussed developing an idea into a product concept in Chapter 3. Here, I want to talk about developing an idea into a project that will prompt people to contribute time, effort, and money to making it happen.

After you get an idea, the next step is to define the project and result. For a weight-loss project, that would be a slimmer, fitter you. For a film project, it would be the movie on the screen. For a construction project, it would be the finished building.

As Stephen Covey said in his bestseller *The Seven Habits of Highly Effective People*, "start with the end in mind." People with an artistic or business vision can see the final product—at least what they think is the final product—in their minds. The result may turn out differently, but the image still serves its purpose, which is to inspire action and guide decisions.

There are various ways to envision the final product. Product prototypes, mentioned in Chapter 3, are one way. In software and services, flow charts show the tasks that the user and the software, or the customer and the business, will perform. Architects' drawings show the design of the buildings and landscapes they and their clients envision. These visual devices make the idea concrete instead of abstract.

TO ACT LIKE A PRODUCER

- generate or find ideas

- plan and schedule the project

- locate and hire the talent

- line up the financing

- oversee the project, budget, and quality

If you tell people about a product, software program, service, or building, you may confuse or bore them. When you show them a visual, you can get their attention.

Development means more than envisioning and depicting the final result, however. It also means charting a path to that result. A movie project is the script and the director, actors, crew, and budget. When these are put together by an agent or independent producer, it's called "packaging." The package includes all the elements that the studio and other parties need in order to make a decision about financing the production of the movie.

The practice of packaging can be exported to other businesses. For example, over the past fifteen years, book packagers have become more important in publishing. A book packager finds an idea or an author with an idea and creates a budget, schedule, and proposal to present to publishers. The packager then oversees the project and, depending on the publisher's needs, delivers a manuscript, an electronic file for the printer, or bound books. Packagers are most often used for coffee-table books, and other books with special production requirements, such as popups, cutouts, or items such as beanbags or other toys.

pack•ag•ing

1. organizing the elements for a film, book, or other product or service, and managing the project to deliver it
2. the overall vision of the project, as in "The idea is good, but it needs packaging"

Once you have a solid idea for the product, service, or business, and of the dimensions of the project, you're ready for preproduction.

Preproduction: Proper Planning Prevents Poor Performance

Preproduction focuses on planning creative ways of budgeting and financing the project, and addressing the logistics and schedule. In this phase, you must also identify and recruit the people you'll need to execute the project. We'll look at these activities in more depth in Part 2 of this book, where we examine the nuts and bolts of "making it real."

Preproduction amounts to an extended planning exercise. You define the results you want to create and the steps you must take to create them. Then you identify the materials, skills, people, and exact amounts of money you will need to take each step. For any project, be sure to budget not only for money, but for time—including other people's time.

Many creative people see planning as boring or unnecessary. They're wrong on both counts. Planning is the act of bringing the future into the present so you can shape the future to your liking. It's not fortunetelling or guesswork. Nor is it assuming that

Take Action

In any idea-driven business, you need to be able to pitch your ideas persuasively. For ways of doing that, see my book, Persuasion, *in this series.*

things will go exactly as you anticipate.

Instead, it's saying, for example, "I'm going to need $7,500 for marketing, and a designer for the Web site and the brochure, and I'm going to need them in four months." That means that you must do certain things, such as raise or save the money and locate the designer so that you have what you need in four months.

Finding Creative Talent

You'll still find many businesses in which everyone who works for the company is on the payroll as an employee. But more people than ever work as freelancers, part-timers, consultants, or entrepreneurs. That means that more people than ever are open to working as independent contractors, especially people in creative fields.

Whatever you are trying to do, from setting up an accounting system to, well, directing a movie, there are people you can hire. Where do you find them? Here are five sources.

---

in•de•pen•dent con•trac•tor

1. a freelance worker; any worker who is not an employee on the organization's payroll
2. any worker who makes himself or herself available for work on projects, or on a part-time basis or for a limited period of full-time work

---

1. *Associations:* There's an association for almost every profession and freelance line of work, and most host Web sites for job postings and members' résumés.

2. *Web sites:* Some sites are dedicated just to bringing independent contractors (and other job seekers) together with those who hire them.

3. *Help-wanted ads:* I've paid for small ads in the *Boston Globe*, my local newspaper, and have always been able to hire good writers for special jobs.

4. *Networking:* This can work faster than other methods because if you trust the recommender, you can locate someone qualified on the first or second try.

5. *Universities:* You can find students educated in the area you need by posting projects in schools that teach the skills your project requires.

Please note that there can be tax and legal implications involved in hiring freelancers and independent contractors.

Production: Managing the People and the Project

The producer organizes all elements of the production and ensures that everything works together to create the intended effects. On the surface, it may look like the producer and director just tell people what to do. Below the surface, however, they're guiding everyone on the project to gener-

Take Action
You must research anything you want to do. For instance, if you want to publish a book, you can learn how to approach agents and editors from sources such as Literary Marketplace *(Writer's Digest Books) and Web sites such as* www.writersdigest.com. *For advertising, you can read* How to Put Your Book together and Get a Job in Advertising, *by Maxine Paetro (Copy Workshop, 2002). There are resources like these for every field.*

ate the perceptions that the movie aims to produce.

The concept of "production values" can help you balance the demands of the product with those of your budget. Some items actually benefit from a bare-bones presentation. For instance, *The Blair Witch Project* had low production values due to necessity, but given the plot and setting, that added to its authenticity.

Slick production values often become an end in and of themselves. For example, in empty but good-looking movies and overproduced, soulless pop music, the bells and whistles can't make up for the lack of substance. This stuff can sell for a while, but rarely is the work of lasting merit. Consider this: The shooting of Steven Spielberg's *Jaws* was hobbled by the fake-looking mechanical shark, which didn't work much of the time. As a result, Spielberg kept the shark off screen for most of the film, which created more suspense than showing it more often would have. As they say, less is more.

The key goal in production is to work within your budget and in service to the product. If the product calls for gritty authenticity, then low production values can work in your favor. For instance, many

pro•duc•tion val•ues

1. the overall look and presentation of a film or other work
2. the level of visual professionalism exhibited in the work

information products with low production values sell at a high price. People will pay $59, $79, and more for loose-leaf material or e-books they want, and often trust the information more than what they would find in a nicely bound book from an established publisher (which can, based on my experience, lead to overpaying in some, but not all, cases).

> " I believe in being an innovator.
>
> —**Walt Disney (founder, The Walt Disney Company)**

Postproduction and Launch: Getting It Out

In postproduction, all the footage that's been shot becomes the raw material to be edited, scored, and shaped into the actual film. At the same time, everything that's needed to launch the movie must be put in place and set in motion. This includes promotional materials ranging from posters and print ads to trailers to show in theaters and on television commercials; the distribution program; and media relations.

The postproduction phase in innovation involves executing the marketing, media, and distribution plans. This means that the elements of a successful launch must be in place before the actual rollout. I'll cover product launch in more depth in Chapter 8. The key parallel between postproduction in the Hollywood model and in innovation is that you have to have all the elements in

"CREATIVES" AND "SUITS" MUST

- Understand each other's talents

- Respect each other's roles

- Meet and talk regularly

- Refrain from demonizing

- Balance budget and quality concerns

place and ready to go. The key differences are that with a product rollout you can do more extensive market testing, roll out the product more gradually, and make adjustments to the product or service even after it's released. You can't do those things with a film or similar project.

INNOVATION IN ACTION

part

2

" NOTHING IS MORE **DANGEROUS** THAN HAVING JUST **ONE IDEA.** **"**

—Emile-Auguste Chartier
(French philosopher
and writer)

Become an Idea Machine

5

Innovators solve problems; the solutions to problems arise as ideas. Successful innovation depends on bringing your best ideas to reality. The more ideas you have, the more good ideas you'll have. Unfortunately, nobody gets only good ideas.

That's why Monsieur Chartier said that there's nothing more dangerous than having just one idea. If you have only one idea, you may believe that idea is the best one—even if it's useless. If it's useless, it's not worth developing, even if it is the best idea you have. So, the more ideas you have to choose from, the better.

This chapter tells you how to generate a lot of ideas. To do that, you first have to forget about whether the ideas are any good. Generate without judging. Then, once you have a bunch of ideas, you can decide which ones are worth developing or at least looking at more closely.

The Battle of the Brains

Your internal critic is the first one to judge your ideas. Allowing the critic to judge the ideas as you are generating them shuts down production, because the critical function overrides the creative function. Generating ideas and judging them are two separate tasks, handled by two different sides of your brain. Basically, the right side of your brain (right hemisphere) engages in creative functions, and the left side (left hemisphere) deals with more logical functions.

L Stands for Logical

I had a hard time remembering which side of the brain performed which functions, so I used a mnemonic device: For the left side think of the letter "L" and link it with "logical" and "legal." Then all that's left is the right side, which is cReative. It's also useful to understand whether you are working on a right-brained or left-brained task, so you can adjust your tools and methods.

The right brain tends to be intuitive, visual, emotional, and open to stimulus. The right side focuses more on the big picture and, when faced with multiple ideas or tasks, deals with them simultaneously. In contrast, the left brain is analytical, verbal, rational, and critical. The left side focuses more on details, and deals with multiple ideas or tasks sequentially. We all use both sides of our brains, but each of us tends to rely more on one side than the other.

Take a moment to consider which side of your brain you favor. Do you avoid reading instructions? Do you jump into a task instead of planning? Do you consider yourself more a "feeler" than a "thinker"? If so, there's a good chance you're right-brained. Artists and musicians and other creative types tend to be right-brained. Do you approach tasks systematically? Instead of jumping in, do you plan a task and take it step by step? Do you consider yourself more a "thinker" than a "feeler"? Accountants and engineers and people drawn to puzzles and pursuits that depend on logic tend to be left-brained. Note that these are informal, stereotypical guidelines that I'm using to make the point.

Take Action
Check out the book Writing on Both Sides of the Brain, *by Henriette Klauser (Perennial Library, 1986), for a good discussion of the hemispheres in your head and some good thinking tools.*

Valuing Both Sides

Neither side of the brain is better than the other. Innovation requires both the right brain and the left brain. The right brain seeks new stimuli, combines things in new ways, generates new ideas, and discovers new solutions. The left brain evaluates and critiques ideas, grapples with practical issues (such as planning the project and preparing a budget), organizes the resources, works out the details, and manages the process.

Problems occur when we fail to value the contribution that each side of the brain makes to innovation. For instance, many right-brained people generate scores of good ideas, but never implement them. They may feel that they're creative, but they shun the practical details of innovation. Some feel underappreciated, when in fact the world desperately needs new ideas. Some of them even blame left-brained people for killing their ideas by pointing out practical obstacles. These folks have to learn to value planning and implementation. Meanwhile, many left-brained people believe that they just aren't creative. Some don't bother trying to innovate, or they kill their ideas before they're hatched. They may see right-brained people as dreamers or rebels and try to kill their ideas. They cultivate a narrow comfort zone and want other people—and their organizations— to stay inside that zone. Many left-brained people have to learn to value imagination and unstructured activities.

What's a person to do?

Pull Them Apart

To win the battle of the brains, separate them. By that, I mean separate the tasks— I'm not recommending a lobotomy. If you separate the tasks in innovation that rely on the right brain from those that rely on the left brain, the two sides can't fight. They may even learn to coexist.

To separate the right- and left-brain tasks, take them step by step. First, generate ideas; then, when you have some ideas, evaluate them. (We'll look at ways of evaluating ideas in Chapter 6.) When you try to judge the ideas as you're getting them, you stop the flow of ideas. Even if you don't shut down the process, you can evaluate an idea better when you focus solely on that task and compare it with other ideas.

There are several tools for generating ideas, the most famous and commonly used being brainstorming. Brainstorming and most other idea-generating techniques keep the left brain at bay while the right brain runs free.

brain•storm

1. to produce ideas quickly, in a group or alone, without judging them

2. to generate as many ideas as possible under time pressure

Thunderheads Unite

Brainstorming is traditionally done in a group, but most people also get good results doing it alone. Usually four to eight people spend thirty seconds to several minutes producing as many ideas as they can on a topic. While the length of time can vary, a brief deadline speeds things along and helps people outrun their internal critics. You can also break a topic into parts and brainstorm in short bursts to keep everyone cranked.

During the session, someone has to take notes or, better still, write the ideas on a flip chart or blackboard. Some groups use index cards, so they can more easily sort the ideas after they are generated.

Almost any open-ended question—that is, one that you can't answer with "yes" or "no"—can work as a topic. Also, the topic can be a statement, such as "Ways of making our products more competitive." Here are a few sample topics:

○ What can we do to make this product easier to use?

○ In what new ways could our customers use our products?

○ How can we lower the cost of producing this product?

○ Ways to get more media attention for our company.

○ Things we can do to solve our customers' inventory (or production or delivery) problems.

There are only two real rules in a brainstorming session:

1. Participants should mention all ideas that come into their heads, no matter how silly or impractical they seem.

2. No one is allowed to criticize anyone's idea.

You'll hear a lot of bad or loopy ideas in a brainstorming session. That's okay. In fact, if you're not coming up with some wacky ideas, you probably aren't really brainstorming. In brainstorming, the goal is quantity, not quality. The more ideas you come up with, the more chance you have of getting some truly new and creative ones.

> If at first the idea is not absurd, then there is no hope for it.
>
> —**Albert Einstein (scientist)**

If You're a Critic, Duck!

Several creativity consultants run brainstorming sessions for companies. To discourage criticism, some of them hand out beanbags or Nerf balls for participants to throw at anyone who criticizes an idea. I've found that it's enough to explain the process and warn people that there's no criticism in brainstorming. Also, I write down all ideas in some form, usually on a flip chart, so everyone knows that every idea is worth reviewing.

Also, remember to use brainstorming on your own. That's best done by opening a blank document on your computer screen, typing the topic at the top, and getting your fingers moving. Or, you can write by hand on a yellow pad or a large sheet of paper. I suppose you could talk into a recording device, but writing seems to stimulate more ideas.

Two More Idea Generators

Here are two other techniques for coming up with ideas:

- Questioning yourself

- Looking up, down, and around

Let's examine each one briefly.

Question Yourself

Another technique is to ask yourself a series of questions directed to the problem you are trying to solve, then answer them. The "Five Ws and an H" traditionally used by journalists is one ready-made set of questions you can use: Who? What? When? Where? Why? How? Always ask "How?" in a business situation: "How can we save the customer's time? How can we help the customer make or save money with our product?" (You can also brainstorm the answer to any question.) Another technique is the "Five Whys." You pick a problem or topic—for example, let's say your company hasn't come up with any new product ideas in the past three years—and then, you ask "why" five times (or more). The

> A major stimulant to creative thinking is focused questions. There is something about a well-worded question that often penetrates to the heart of the matter and triggers new ideas and insights.
>
> —Brian Tracy (author and motivational speaker)

goal is to get to the bottom of things. For example:

- ○ Problem: We haven't developed any new products in the past three years.

- ○ Why?

- ○ It hasn't been a priority.

- ○ Why?

- ○ We've focused on moving into new markets with our current products.

- ○ Why?

- ○ Growth topped out in our old markets.

- ○ Why?

- ○ We don't know.

- ○ Why?

- ○ We haven't done any research or analyzed that situation.

This would probably lead the group to conclude that they should research the reasons for lack of growth in their old markets.

Four Ways to Find Problems

To solve problems, you have to know where to look for them and recognize a good one when you see one. What's a good problem? One that you might be able to solve with a solution you can sell. Here are four places to look for problems to solve:

Look for Information Gaps

Things I wish I'd thought of: Places Rated, The 100 Best Companies to Work For, and every guide to doing your income taxes. This is basic information that people need, and it changes often, which means they buy an update almost every year.

Choose Information Markets Carefully

The more desperately people need information, the more they will pay for it. That's why courses that guarantee high scores on college entrance and bar exams can charge so much. People hate paying for low-need information, which the Internet offers free. To succeed as an "infopreneur" you're usually better off with a small market that has a high need for information rather than a large market with a low need.

For our purposes, information encompasses books, articles, e-books, and guides; research, training, education, conferences, and consulting; specific types of coaching via Internet, telephone, and in person; newsletters, studies, surveys, and bulletins on industries, technologies, and professions; and everything published by government agencies, investment companies, and associations.

To become an "infopreneur" ask yourself:

- *What do I know that other people need or want to know? Can my expertise or one of my ongoing interests support a newsletter or Web site?*

- *Where and how can I access or compile information, either from secondary sources, such as government agencies or public records, or from primary sources, such as surveys that I can conduct or have someone conduct?*

- *Who wants to get information out to the public or to specialized audiences? How can I help them do that for a fee?*

- *Where does information change more often than it's updated? Would anyone pay for more current information? Could I update it cheaply and accurately, perhaps via the Internet?*

- *What information of my own can I repurpose for other media or audiences? Have I written articles that can become a book or an e-book? Have I written a book that can spawn articles? Do I have material that would work on a Web site?*

TO FIND OPPORTUNI-TIES, LOOK FOR

- *Information gaps you can fill*

- *Businesses you can standardize*

- *Products or services you can improve*

- *Social and business trends*

Look for Things to Standardize

A good chunk of ServiceMaster's $3 billion in annual sales comes from three basic businesses that every homeowner needs: lawn maintenance (TruGreen ChemLawn), house-cleaning (Merry Maids), and pest control (Terminix). Companies like these lower the risk of dealing with local businesses known for uneven performance. They provide standard training, procedures, uniforms, supplies, and advertising to businesses that were once mom-and-pop operations. Almost every franchise or chain—Burger King, Roto-Rooter, True Value Hardware, CVS, 7-Eleven, Century 21, and Holiday Inn, to name only a few—uses these principles.

Franchise or Chain?

Franchising is a specialized area of business. In a franchise, the franchisee buys the right to use the logo, products, and practices of the franchising company, and they share the profits. In a chain, a company owns the locations and hires managers. Some companies use both franchises and company-owned locations. In good franchises, both parties share the risks and rewards. In bad ones, the company overcharges its franchisees for supplies and hogs the profits.

You may think that starting a franchise or chain lies beyond you, but they all started small—usually with one location—and, as noted, many are in very basic businesses. Most franchises and chains rely on innovative branding and marketing coupled with sound management. Indeed, some companies simply seek businesses that they can turn into franchises.

Look for Things to Copy

Some innovations aren't terribly innovative. In fact, knockoffs—or, to use the more genteel term, parity products—have a long history of success. When Toyota introduced its Lexus line of luxury cars, Nissan was close behind with Infiniti. When IDG's Dummies series took off, Alpha Books soon introduced the Complete Idiot's Guide series. Every rock band or pop singer that copies the originator of a style is a knockoff.

Anything successful—toothpaste with whiteners, ketchup with hot sauce, handbags with hardware, small stereo systems, reality TV shows, soft contact lenses—will soon be copied. That's why every innovation soon faces competitors.

But don't patent and copyright laws prohibit ripping off ideas? Yes, but in limited ways. In general, you can't patent or copyright an idea—only the expression of the idea. So, you can't patent the idea of, say, a minivan. In fact, there's nothing to stop another car company from taking apart a competitor's minivan, seeing how it works, and then making its own, in a process known as reverse engineering. Copying the exact design and construction isn't permitted, but small changes usually don't affect the product's appearance or performance.

re•verse en•gi•neer•ing

1. taking apart a product to see how it is made and how it works
2. copying a competing product's function and design, with small, legal changes

Look for Trends

Successful products and services often capitalize on trends. Trends are usually temporary changes in people's attitudes and behavior due to social, demographic, political, and economic developments. Here are several trends and the products and services that have resulted:

trend

1. usually, long- or short-term change in attitudes or behavior among people
2. changes rooted in social, demographic, political, or economic developments
3. attitudes or behaviors that can be expected to change in some way

○ *Rising environmental concerns—The refuse and effluvia produced by 6-billion-plus people are going to pollute a planet. It's that simple. People will notice it and get ideas for things like recyclable packaging, biodegradable detergents, and organizations that protect beleaguered wildlife.*

○ *Increasing health concerns— When movie stars like Humphrey Bogart and Steve McQueen die before their time due to drinking liquor and smoking cigarettes, people question the glamour of those activities. They switch to white wine and gumdrops. When a third of the population is overweight, Slim-Fast will sell.*

○ *Aging of the baby boomers—People tire of hearing about the baby boomers because marketers never tire of selling to 76 million people who all have pretty much the same needs at the same time. Boomers needed* apartments, so cities were renovated. They needed houses, so suburbs expanded. Soon, they're going to need retirement communities—not to mention health care, investment income, and RVs. This population cohort, often described as "the pig in the python," has moved through the demographic tables, fueling buying binges for whatever it is that people need at a certain age.

○ Pendulum trends—Many popular entertainment trends periodically reverse themselves. The bland pop music of the mid-1950s set the stage for Elvis Presley. The puppy-love romanticism of the early 1960s gave rise to Bob Dylan and the Beatles and the Stones. Efforts to top that gave us Led Zeppelin and pompous heavy metal bands. In retaliation, the Ramones and punk bands stripped things down. Then hair bands "repompousified" it until Nirvana and grunge made it real again. Television, movie, and fashion trends follow similar patterns, moving to one extreme and then reversing until reaching the other. Thus, the Next Big Thing may be a return to, or an update of, the Same Old Thing.

○ Technology trends—One key trend has been the fragmentation of the media audience due to cable and satellite TV (and radio), and the Internet, iPod, and other new media. Even into the 1980s, people mainly watched three major networks. That audience has shattered, perhaps for the foreseeable future

KEY TRENDS TO WATCH

○ Environmental concerns

○ Alternative energy sources

○ Health, fitness, and organic foods

○ Aging of the population

○ Cocooning and connecting via technology

*(whatever that is). Experts argue about
whether people are now more isolated
or more connected, but it's clear that
the mass media isn't what it used to be,
except on Super Bowl Sunday.*

In the political thriller *Three Days of the
Condor*, two operatives are talking about
the hero, and one asks the other where
the hero learned evasive moves. The other
operative answers that "he reads everything." I can't think of a better way to never
run out of ideas.

An Ounce of Protection

Finally, there is the issue of establishing
ownership of your innovation. In the United
States, the three major tools for establishing ownership rights in inventions, innovations, and intellectual properties are patents, trademarks, and copyrights.

A patent confirms ownership of the
invention of a process, machine, item,
or formulation (such as a chemical com-
pound), or the design for an item, or the
development of a new variety of plant.

A trademark confirms ownership of
words, symbols, sounds, or colors that
distinguish a product or service. A service
mark is a trademark for a service rather
than for a product. Brands and logos are
subject to trademarks.

A copyright confirms ownership of a piece of writing, software, music, or work of art.

The type of protection and process for establishing ownership varies for each tool. There are also other means of protecting intellectual property, the most common being certain legal agreements. The sources for much of this material are the Web sites of the United States Patent and Trademark Office, with the homepage *www.uspto.gov*, and the United States Copyright Office, with the homepage *www.copyright.gov*.

" THE DIFFICULTY LIES NOT SO MUCH IN **DEVELOPING NEW IDEAS** AS IN ESCAPING FROM OLD ONES. **"**

—John Maynard Keynes
(British economist)

Taking Ideas to the Next Level

6

Ideas are potentially the most valuable thing you can have. The key word here is potentially. Some people like their ideas so much that they become enamored of them. They love an idea for the idea itself. Innovators consider an idea to be raw material. Raw material, like raw land, must be developed to become profitable.

People who consider the idea itself as the end product don't develop their ideas. Often, these people are very creative, but they are also the people who occasionally see a new product, service, film, or book and say, "You know, I had that idea three years ago." Yes, they had the idea, but so did someone else, and someone else developed the idea into an innovation.

> Ideas won't keep. Something must be done about them.
>
> **—Alfred North Whitehead (British mathematician and philosopher)**

In this chapter, we look at ways to take the raw material of ideas to the next level—the process of developing the idea.

While Lord Keynes is right about old ideas, developing new ones does take some effort. This means testing ideas to find the best one, then enriching it, and shaping it into the actual product or service. In Chapter 5, we looked at ways of generating ideas. Here we look at developing them, which is the first thing to do with an idea after you've got it.

Get Moving

First, I have a word of caution. Actually, three words of caution: Don't waste time. If you have an idea that you know is worth developing, get moving. Start developing it right away. Don't commit huge amounts of time or money to the idea—at least not right away. Instead, if you like and believe in the idea, start developing it. When you do begin development, your belief in the idea will be reinforced, or not. If it is reinforced, great. You and the idea are on your way. If not, that's okay; on to the next!

But don't sit there believing in your idea's potential without doing anything about it. Thanks to the Internet, information travels very freely today. Most people who are curious in a given sphere have access to the same information. They also face the same problems. So, they are going to be working on the same problems with the same information.

So, what's going to happen if you hesitate to get started on your idea, while others are accessing the same information? Others are going to get similar ideas. It's called "simultaneous invention." When that happens, the person or company that has the better idea or gets to market first—or both—will win. To get moving, start developing the idea.

While good ideas often come from one person, it really takes the varied viewpoints and skills of a team to develop them.

si•mul•ta•ne•ous in•ven•tion

1. two or more parties working separately and developing the same innovation (examples include the automobile and the bicycle)
2. similar discoveries resulting from similar scientific research at about the same time

Try an Idea Generation Program

The ideas that I'm talking about developing in this chapter result from brainstorming and other idea generation methods. These include the ideas you get by listening to your salespeople and tracking your competitors, as I suggested in Chapter 3, and from the methods I presented in Chapter 5.

One potential source I haven't mentioned is employee idea generation programs. These programs, usually run by the marketing department, solicit product ideas from the entire staff. It's one of the

AN IDEA GENERATION CAMPAIGN SHOULD

- Encourage ideas from everyone

- Use a standard form for submitting ideas

- Offer rewards for ideas that are used

- Notify people of the decision on their ideas

uses of the suggestion boxes that many companies hang in their hallways or cafeterias. However, the suggestion box system doesn't prompt many new product ideas. It's too general and unfocused, and people are prone to suggesting things that management would, uh, rather not do.

Low Odds, High Returns

In my experience at D&B Credit Services, out of a hundred ideas we would screen out about eighty to ninety, evaluate the remaining ten to twenty, and concept-test three in order to develop one product. That reflects the reality I described in Chapter 5: You need a lot of ideas to get a good one. Many of the ideas that people submitted were not well thought-out, even though we issued guidelines for them to consider.

A new product idea program explicitly asks people for new ideas. These programs also ask for ideas for cutting costs or improving work methods. Soliciting those ideas isn't bad, although it does pull the focus off new products. Whichever system you use, be sure follow these guidelines:

IDEA PROGRAM GUIDELINES

○ Be sure the chief executive encourages all employees to submit ideas in an annual memo, with reminders two or three times a year.

- Explain the procedure for submitting ideas—for instance, on a hard copy or electronic form or via e-mail.

- Tell employees that all ideas will be acknowledged and considered, and that they will hear about the outcome.

- Offer a cash prize for any idea that leads to a new product, either a lump sum of, say, $10,000 or $25,000, or a small percentage of the first year's revenue.

Usually a small percentage of employees contributes ideas, most of which are not usable, and that's to be expected. But they do generate ideas. Those ideas sometimes spark even better ideas in the minds of those who evaluate the results of the program.

Time to Get Critical

In Chapter 5, I asked you not to criticize ideas as you generate them because you'll curtail the creative process. That time is now past. Once you have ideas, you want to find the best ones and put them to work. How do you do that?

Most companies and many creative teams use a two-step process for judging ideas. First they screen the ideas,

screen

1. to apply criteria to ideas or proposals (or anything) to judge their suitability
2. to determine whether or not an item continues in a process
3. the criteria themselves, as in "We need a finer screen"

and then they evaluate the remaining ones. Screening is a form of evaluation, but it's a first-level critique rather than a detailed evaluation. Basically, you are screening out the ones that you immediately see as non-starters. For instance, you screen out ideas that are silly, illegal, unethical, or outside the scope of your business. You also screen out any that are clearly impractical, way too expensive, or technologically unfeasible.

When you have screened out the ideas you can't use, you evaluate those that remain and select the best ones for further development. This second-level critique takes more time because it's a process of selection rather than rejection. It's also a logical way to proceed. It takes more time and effort to evaluate something carefully than to reject it. Devote that time and effort only to ideas that may become marketable products.

A good idea, at least for a mass-market consumer product, is usually simple enough for a relatively uneducated person to grasp. Always try to make your idea as clear as you can.

You'll get the best results when you screen and evaluate ideas with a group of people using standard criteria. The group should include people of different backgrounds, and ideally someone from each department involved in developing, producing, marketing, and selling the product. If you're a solo entrepreneur, you should have a few people with varied experience who act as a formal or informal, paid or unpaid advisory board to help with these kinds of decisions.

Go Hire an Idea

Idea screening and evaluation resembles the hiring process. When managers review résumés, cover letters, and applications, they first screen out candidates who are clearly unqualified because they write poorly or lack the required education or experience. Then, the manager carefully evaluates the remaining résumés, and calls in some of those candidates for interviews. In any situation in which people must judge a large number of things, they first eliminate, then evaluate.

Here Are Sample Criteria

Standard criteria are characteristics that the group develops and agrees to beforehand. These are written criteria and should be set up as an online or hard-copy form. For example, here are six criteria for screening new product ideas:

1. Does the idea fit our overall mission and business strategy?

Yes   No

2. Does the product fill an identified need of our current customers?

Yes   No

3. Does the product fill an identified need for new customers we have targeted?

Yes   No

4. Could we develop the product with our existing resources?

       Yes   No

5. Could we sell and deliver the product through our existing distribution channels?

       Yes   No

6. Does the potential annual revenue exceed our established minimum?

       Yes   No

These questions relate to basic issues in the decision to pursue a product idea. First, you want to develop only ideas that fit your mission and business strategy (Question #1). Assuming your outfit has a clear, useful strategy, everything your company does should support it.

Second, the product had better fill a need for current or new customers, or you won't be able to sell it (Questions #2 and #3).

Third, if you can make and sell the product with existing resources, that's something in its favor (Questions #4 and #5). This doesn't mean that you should pursue *only* ideas for products that you can make and sell with existing resources. It's just that those products require less investment in new resources and take less time to develop.

Finally, most companies expect some minimum level of revenue from a new product (Question #6). This varies with the size of the company; for example, to a billion-dollar company, an idea with annual revenue potential of $500,000 might be unacceptable, but to a $5 million company, it probably would be attractive.

There are many ways of defining and wording screening criteria. Some companies use numerous criteria and divide them into production, marketing, and financial items. Many companies use a scoring system that assigns different weights to different criteria. Then each participant in the screening rates each idea on each criterion (say, from one to five), multiplies by the weight, and then calculates a final score. Then, the team can compare scores objectively.

The key is to have a group use a standard method of screening ideas and deciding which ones go to the next step (the evaluation). Even during screening, however, people should discuss the ideas. They might often agree unanimously on the obviously bad ideas. However, because people with different backgrounds bring different perspectives to the exercise, someone may see a reason to pursue an idea that others would reject. That person's views should be heard and considered.

> Exhilaration is that feeling you get just after a great idea hits you and just before you realize what's wrong with it.
>
> —Anonymous

Look Closer: Idea Evaluation

When you have screened out the ideas you can't use, you apply a finer filter to those that remain. This means examining each idea more closely, and applying more sophisticated criteria.

The two overarching questions are "How large an opportunity does the product idea represent, and how feasible is it for us to develop this product and bring it to market?" Another way of expressing them is, "How much could we make selling this product? How much would it cost to produce and sell it?"

Almost all of the criteria and any analysis at this point should help to answer those questions. The following are some specific issues you must consider.

MARKET SIZE AND CHARACTERISTICS

- How urgent and widespread is the problem that this product solves?

- How many organizations, households, or individuals have this problem? Is this a problem only in our domestic market, or in international markets too?

- How large is the potential market? (That is, how many people would pay for the solution?)

- How would we market, sell, and distribute the product?

- Who are the Innovators, Early Adopters, Early Majority, Late Majority, and Laggards with regard to this product? Can we sell to the Innovators and Early Adopters?

- How much of the market could we realistically capture in the first year after product launch? The second year? Over the life of the product?

THE REVENUE OPPORTUNITY

- How costly is the problem that the product solves?

- What would customers realistically pay for this product? Would some customers pay more than others?

- Is it a one-time or repeat purchase? How often would a customer use and purchase the product?

- Is this a single product or a potential product line? Are there opportunities to sell add-ons, services, maintenance, or parts?

- What total revenue do we project for the first year after product launch? The second year? Over the life of the product?

- How much would we have to spend to develop this product?

- How much would we have to invest in real estate and equipment to produce and deliver this product?

- What costs do we project for materials and human resources (including training and benefits) to make the product?

- Subtracting the development costs, investment, and costs from our revenue, how much profit do we project for the first year, second year, and so on, over the life of the product?

- Can we develop the product and outsource the design and production of it? What costs would be associated with doing that?

These are not exhaustive lists of questions. In fact, I've simplified the financial decisions here, because the analytical tools needed to make them are beyond the scope of this book. Those tools include calculating investments and profits so you can compare new products. For example, the internal rate of return tells you the rate that you'd earn on the money invested in the product. The payback period tells you the number of months or years it would take to earn back the amount invested. You can learn how to do these calculations from various sources, including my book *The Complete Idiot's Guide to MBA Basics.*

Do We Continue?

The next step—actually concept-testing the idea—is still a relatively small, low-risk part of the development process. That is, it's small relative to the entire product development process. In some situations or companies, you would first draw up the business case or a business plan for the product. That document would answer the questions posed in the previous section and explain why development should continue. In other situations, development would continue based on the positive evaluation of the idea.

To Test or Not to Test?

I remind you that this development process applies as much to ideas for services as it does to ideas for products, and to entrepreneurs and small businesses as well as to large companies. Entrepreneurs can become so fired up about an idea that they don't bother concept-testing it, and some prepare only the sketchiest financial projections.

I realize that some ideas have proven to be so terrific, or the business was so basic, that the entrepreneur could jump in, work like a demon, and succeed. It's also true that people with a strong vision—for instance, Ben Cohen and Jerry Greenfield, the founders of Ben & Jerry's Ice Cream—or a dream, such as owning a restaurant, will move forward and make the idea work based on their knowledge, skills, and commitment. Some businesses literally start with something as simple as a recipe for salad dressing. That is the actual case of Newman's Own, which started with actor and philanthropist Paul Newman's oil-and-vinegar salad dressing, originally distributed in wine bottles to his friends at Christmastime.

Be Conservative

It's my experience that people can easily become overly optimistic about the size of the potential market for a product. To be conservative, you might project that in the first year you will capture about 3 percent of the market (that is, the Innovators from Rogers's technology adoption curve, explained in Chapter 2) or 10 to 15 percent over the next one to two years. Never make the mistake of believing that you will capture the entire potential market over the life of the product.

Most of us, though, will do best by testing product ideas and researching the size of the market. It's a must in any corporate environment, and for any entrepreneur who wants to raise money. (I'll cover early-stage businesses in Chapter 11.)

How do you develop an idea? How do you make it bigger, richer, and more attractive? You use information and imagination.

Developing an Idea into a Concept

To develop an idea into a concept, envision how it would look and work. Start to imagine design elements. Think about form and function, and which might be more important. Designers figure out how things should look. That's form. Engineers figure out how things should work. That's function. In most cases, you need a product that looks good and works well.

I say "in most cases" advisedly. Many people believe that form should always follow function. If you've seen $400 shoes by Jimmy Choo and Manolo Blahnik, you know that form, even at the expense of function, can sometimes carry the day (that is, unless women actually aren't supposed to walk, or stand, in those shoes). The early versions of the fire-breathing Dodge Viper had no side windows or outside door handles—and the car cost north of $60,000!

But most products, and certainly any product aimed at businesses, have to be easy to use and work correctly. Think about how the product would work and how the

Take Action
Visit www.debonogroup .com *to learn about the work of Edward de Bono, author of* Six Thinking Hats *and other books on creativity.*

customer would use it. How important is the way it looks? How important is durability? How would you get it produced? What about storage, packaging, and shipping?

If it's a service, imagine when customers would need it and how they would initiate a request. They might request it with a phone call (to whom?), a visit to a Web site (with what kind of interface?), or with an e-mail. How would they receive the service? In person, over the phone, or via the Web? Do they have to leave the house? Does your company or a third party deliver the actual service? How would you know whether customers received the service, and whether they got what they wanted?

In all cases, the chief concern is whether the product or service solves the customer's problem in the way that it should.

Conduct a Concept Test

For most concept testing, you don't need a huge sample. If you test a product concept with twenty potential customers and eighteen say they love it, you probably don't need more research to determine that you're going to continue developing the product. Of course, you have to ensure that the sample fairly represents the larger market. You can't just ask the most likely customers and assume that their responses apply to all your customers.

Don't spend a lot of time and resources trying to create the perfect prototype. Get something in front of potential customers and gather their responses. It's easy to let perfectionism rule the day, but the real priority is getting a good number of ideas out there so you can see what works.

The Price Is Right?

In a concept test, you'll be tempted to ask how much respondents might pay for the product. It's hard enough to gauge buying intentions. People often say, "This product is great," and then, when asked if they'd buy it, add, "for someone else." You can ask about the price they might pay, but don't place much stock in the answers. (You can get a fix on pricing later, during the market test.)

Testing product concepts on the Web can be extremely cost-effective, although it can be hard to reach exactly the people you want, particularly if you're trying to move into a new market. On the other hand, if you have a good level of Web-site traffic or e-newsletter readers, you can briefly describe the concept and invite people to take the concept test. The number of click-throughs is itself a measure of people's interest in the product idea.

Finally, be sure to limit the number of questions in the concept test, especially in Web-based surveys. People have limited time for this sort of thing, so ask the most important question first, and respect their time. Don't constantly return to the same respondents unless you know they are interested. Survey fatigue is so widespread that market research companies must often contact five, ten, or more potential respondents to get one to take part in a lengthy survey.

Setting up the Concept Test

Telephone or e-mail a mix of customers if possible. You want to ask people who you think will be interested in the concept, but include a few who might not be. Those people might point out things that the others wouldn't, just because they'll be more skeptical of the concept in general.

However you explain or represent the product or service concept—description, mockup, prototype, or simulation—be sure the respondents understand it. If possible, test their understanding with a question about the way the product or service works.

Be sure to ask the same questions in the same way to respondents. Don't appear too eager to get a positive response.

Questions to Ask in a Concept Test

In a concept test, aim to learn what respondents think of the product idea. Ask questions such as these:

Take Action
You can use the Internet to gauge an idea's potential with the keyword search statistics of a few search engines. Go to https://adwords.google.com *to see Google's version of this tool. The more searches, the more interest in that area.*

- *Do you understand the product and how it works? Do you have questions about it?*

- *Which features of the product strike you as the most important? The least important?*

- *What, if anything, do you think this product would help you do?*

- *How do you go about doing these things now?*

- *What specific benefits do you see the product offering you?*

- *Have you ever felt the need for this product or service in the past?*

- *How often do you think you would use the product?*

- *What barriers do you see to using the product?*

- *What other comments do you have about the product?*

CONCEPT-TESTING HINTS

- *Tell respondents that you want their honest opinions*

- *Know the respondent's type on the technology adoption curve*

- *Keep questions short and to the point*

- *Don't overwhelm respondents with dozens of questions*

- *Don't go to the same respondents too often, or you'll wear them out*

Kill Bad Ideas Fast

Kill the bad as soon as possible, because the more that's invested in development, the harder it becomes to discontinue a product or service. Be dispassionate and let the data from the concept test and other analysis do the talking. Solid work in these early stages saves huge amounts of resources later.

" AH, **GOOD TASTE!** WHAT A DREADFUL THING! TASTE IS THE **ENEMY** OF **CREATIVENESS.** "

—Pablo Picasso
(artist and sculptor)

Designing and Testing Innovative Products

7

An innovation is the physical form of an idea—a new product or service—and once you get into physical form, you must consider design. Design determines how something will look, feel, and work. It also affects cost, materials, safety, manufacturability, storage, distribution, and delivery. All of those factors feed into construction, into how the product will be built.

In this chapter, I will present basic design issues for innovators to consider. Then, we'll look at how to get the most from product and market testing. I'll discuss options for actually getting the product produced in Chapter 9.

> Good design is making something intelligible and memorable. Great design is making something memorable and meaningful.
>
> —**Dieter Rams**
> **(industrial designer)**

People Buy Design

The term "design" can be applied to anything from an orange crate to the Sydney Opera House. Every object or system possesses a design—an underlying plan for construction and function. Thus the topic of design is as broad and varied as are classes of products and services. Specific principles inform the design of specific things, giving rise to such design disciplines as automotive, software, interior, fashion, packaging, architectural, and instructional, among many others.

A Case of Vodka

Differences among vodkas exist, but they are small given that vodka consists mainly of alcohol diluted with water. So, the bottle has become a major differentiator, commanding significant design resources. As Forbes.com points out, "Some, like Vox and Ciroc, go for high-concept, ultra-hip bottle shapes. Some hire famous designers. Wyborowa even went so far as to commission celebrity architect Frank Gehry for its bottle." Advertising helps, but the bottle is the brand.

Design also refers more narrowly to the aesthetic values that inform an object's form and function. In other words, in addition to making something easy and safe to use (function), design renders it pleasing to the eye and touch (form).

Think about products you enjoy looking at. For me these include the Corvette and the VW Beetle; almost anything made by Apple, Braun, or Herman Miller; the Finlandia bottle; the original Marlboro box; and cap toe dress shoes. Clearly, design preferences involve taste. As the saying goes, there's no accounting for taste; yet, products draw attention and sales on the basis of their design. Services also must be consciously and carefully designed.

Innovators must at least consider design, partly because quality is now the "price of admission" to most markets, and differences in product performance are usually small. Good design itself can give a company a competitive advantage. Design won't compensate for poor performance or construction flaws; in fact, performance and construction are basic design considerations. However, design can get a product noticed and purchased, and can communicate the brand message.

brand mes·sage

1. look and feel of a product's packaging and advertising
2. social and psychological values communicated by a company or product, such as prestige, economy, or environmental friendliness
3. brand identity

Getting Design Right

Good design makes a product appealing to the senses and easy to use, maintain, and store. It makes the product safe and even fun to use. It also differentiates the product from others of its type. Automotive design is of paramount importance given that, from the engineering standpoint, most cars will move us down the road safely at remarkable speeds. Indeed, design is a major differentiator for products as prosaic as vacuum cleaners, toothbrushes, and kitchen appliances.

However, design considerations go well beyond a product's appearance and appeal to include:

- Customers' expectations and desires as expressed in the concept test and other research

- Cost of materials, assembly, packaging, transportation, storage, and, if applicable, installation

- Durability, maintenance, repairs, parts availability, and service technicians' skills

- Environmental and safety regulations, and product liability issues

- Degree to which customization of the product or service will be permitted, if at all

All of these considerations must be addressed in the design stage. One of the key tools for doing this is customer requirements, which designers translate into design specifications, typically with the help of engineers. We'll look at customer requirements and design specifications later in this chapter.

For now, think about the considerations in the previous list as we examine the three major design concerns for a product: functionality, aesthetics, and manufacturability.

Functionality: Design It to Work

The product must do what it's supposed to do. If the unit has a motor, it must be powerful enough to run the unit, the housing large enough to hold the motor, and all parts sufficiently heat resistant. If a spice rack is supposed to hold little bottles of spices, it should hold them so that you can remove one bottle without knocking others off the rack. If the car is meant to be driven at 140 miles per hour—on a closed track, of course—it should handle well at those speeds.

Have you ever looked at something and wondered, "Why did they put that switch there? Why do you have to take this off to get to that screw?" Although it may be bad design, it might not be the designers' fault. They may have had to make compromises in the design, or maybe they lost an argument with the engineers or production people. However it happened, the resulting design is bad if the ergonomics are poor or routine repairs are onerous.

er·go·nom·ics

1. study of interactions between humans and a physical system
2. design considerations related to the safety and comfort of products

Take Action
*Learn more about ergo-
nomics at* www.iea.cc,
*the official Web site of the
International Ergonomics
Association.*

In certain product and service categories, some people will forgive functional design flaws. They will tolerate cramped sports cars, uncomfortable shoes, and restaurants with rude waiters in order to see themselves as stylish. However, it's not a good idea to bet on your customers doing so.

So, from the functional standpoint, the product should:

○ *Do what it is supposed to do and perform to expectations*

○ *Be safe and easy to use, or at least not unnecessarily dangerous or difficult*

○ *Have all the parts that it requires to perform its function—no more, no fewer*

○ *Not sacrifice function to form, without a very good reason*

Let's face it, though—the product should still look good.

Aesthetics: Design It to Look Good

We've all heard the phrase, "It's not pretty, but it'll do the job." Sometimes that's okay, but usually it's not. Take a look at the competition and your product category. In general, if you're in a truly utilitarian product category, you may not need to spend much time thinking about appearances. The basic design of many items, such as hammers, nails, books, and eggs, really can't be improved. (Watch someone make a liar of me!)

Again, it all depends on your product or service category and your target markets. Whatever you decide about the design of your product, bear in mind that stylish goes out of style, but real style doesn't.

What might be termed timeless style hews to certain design principles, which include:

- *Blending form and function, rather than sacrificing one to the other*

- *Balancing the visual elements rather than exaggerating them*

- *Using graceful lines, whether bold or understated, and colors that excite or soothe, in keeping with the product's purpose (red Corvette, black Mercedes)*

- *Eschewing garishness and attention-seeking for their own sakes*

- *Achieving harmony with the surroundings or environment in which the item will be used, without necessarily just blending in*

Manufacturability: Design It to Be Made

One of the great contributions of designers over the past century was well-designed mass-produced products. From the early days of modern manufacturing, many companies employed designers to develop products that worked well and looked good and could be manufactured at a reasonable cost.

When it comes to designing a product for manufacturability, several considerations move to the fore, including:

○ *Quality assurance issues, meaning that the product must be built as specified over all production runs*

○ *Production issues, which include the steps in the production process, perform-or-outsource decisions, and necessary equipment, facilities, and skills*

○ *Financial issues, such as the cost of labor, materials, plant, and equipment, the price of the product, and the projected sales and profits*

○ *Product line issues, such as number of models to produce, subsequent versions, and special orders or custom-built versions*

○ *Distribution issues, which include packaging, storage, shipping, display, waste, shelf life, breakage, and theft*

Take Action

Browse www.design museum.org *(especially* www.designmuseum.org/ design/index*), which is the site of the Design Museum, and* www.dmi.org, *the site of the Design Management Institute, for ideas, information, and articles on design and design management.*

In other words, product design must ensure that the product not only works well and looks good, but can also be produced at a cost that makes sense for the price the company can charge.

Customer Requirements and Design Specifications

Function, aesthetics, and manufacturability come together in drawings and descriptions known as product requirements and specifications. In general, requirements define what a product or service needs to do, while specifications define how the product must be built or the service configured in order to do it. For example, customer requirements are what the customer needs a product to do. Functional specifications would identify the features, materials, and construction details, such as size and weight, that will enable the product to meet those requirements.

You define requirements through concept testing, product testing, and other market research; by reviewing customer complaints and warranty claims; and by observing customers' experiences. You define specifications by applying the relevant design and engineering principles to the product, which is detailed, specialized work.

Specifications enable you to produce a product that will meet the customers' needs. The specifications are communicated to production managers in your company or to a contract manufacturer, and they build the product to the specs. The more clearly and carefully defined the specifications, the better your chances of getting the product you envisioned.

Designing Services

Most services contain human labor in some direct form, rather than subsuming it in the product. The service may comprise manual labor, intellectual labor, or both. Many services rely on human and machine (or computerized) labor, while others, such as telecommunications, rely very heavily on machines and computers.

The point is this: People's interactions with customers are harder to control than a machine or computer. Service design must carefully define the deliverables and the actions required to create them, and the necessary skills of the people performing those actions. The more complex, expensive, and important the deliverables are, the more skill your people will require.

Let's say you have an innovative way of doing financial planning. Let's say it uses your software to integrate data from public sources with the client's financial information on a weekly or daily basis, and you'll provide financial consulting as well. Let's say you want to start one office with a partner and build the business into a regional financial planning powerhouse in five years.

Now, well before you write your business plan (which I discuss in Chapter 11), you must design your service, which involves:

- Considering what you will actually deliver. The deliverables might include a periodically updated budget and financial plan, the software system, public information, personal and telephone consultations, and perhaps buy-and-sell recommendations

- Defining the sales process and the broad process for service delivery, which includes meetings with the client, gathering and analyzing information, identifying the client's various goals, and helping the client reach those goals through budgeting, saving, and investing

- Identifying the human, computer, and information resources the service will require, including the skills and training you and your planners will need,

licensing requirements, computer
equipment, and communication
services

○ Creating the actual service design,
which brings together all elements
visually and in written policies and
procedures: staffing and equipment
requirements; specified interfaces and
handoffs among salespeople, financial planners, and clients; requirements for the billing system;
and methods of troubleshooting

Service design doesn't just happen. If
you observe the service providers you deal
with in your life, you'll see who's working
within a well-designed delivery system
and who isn't.

Many companies that do a good job of
designing their product or service completely fail to design their sales process.
Think of sales as a service, and design a
process that moves the customer through
that process.

While individual performance will
always affect levels of service, a well-
designed system will deliver the best service most consistently.

EXAMPLES OF SERVICES

○ Business services,
including advertis-
ing and employ-
ment agencies,
consulting firms,
and industrial
cleaning

○ Personal services,
such as hairstyl-
ing, pedicures,
trainers, and
shoppers

○ Health care,
which includes
everything from
immunizations to
brain surgery

○ Travel, hospitality,
restaurants, and
car rental

Product Testing

As noted in Chapter 3, the product test
gauges how well the product or service
works for the customer. You are testing

the product's design, instructions, performance, usage, quality, and durability. Various products are tested in various ways. The key is to test them among real customers and under real conditions, keeping these guidelines in mind:

A Service Needs Something to Sell

If you ever set up shop as a consultant, be sure to define a clear deliverable. Expertise in technology, marketing, sales, or human resources isn't enough. You must define exactly what you're going to do for clients—including the projects you envision, the access and information you'll need, what you will do, and what the client will receive. Without those things, you're just holding yourself out as a smart person who maybe can help.

- Plan the test carefully, rather than just giving it to a few customers to use and then interviewing them later. Know what you want to test; develop ways to measure those things; set up ways of obtaining and analyzing the information you need from customers.

- For business-to-business (B-to-B) products and services, be sure to test compatibility with current operations and identify any changes that customers must make in order to use the product.

- If the product is complex, realistically gauge the amount of instruction, training, and support that customers will need. This holds true for consumer, as well as B-to-B, products.

Take Action
Browse the Web site of
Decision Analyst, Inc. (www
.decisionanalyst.com),
for good information on
product testing.

○ Note the features that users like and
dislike; enhance the former and fix or
eliminate the latter.

○ Notice instances of misuse and danger. To avoid product liability lawsuits,
eliminate dangers or minimize them,
and warn users appropriately.

A few rounds of product testing might
be useful, if you have the luxury of developing several iterations of the product
based on input from test participants.

Product Liability a Problem?

Some 40,000 product liability lawsuits are filed in the United
States annually. While this is a small portion of the 20 million civil suits filed annually, companies must take product
safety seriously. In a federal suit, tobacco companies were
held liable for lung disease because the product—cigarettes—was harmful when used for its intended purpose.

You can anticipate and "design around"
some dangers. In many car models, the igni-
tion key can't be removed until the trans-
mission has been shifted into park. This has
reduced the number of cars that roll down
hills after the driver exits the vehicle.

Market Testing

As you'll recall from Chapter 3, market testing attempts to measure buying behavior in
various market segments. Usually, you are

testing the participants' purchase volume and price sensitivity.

Done correctly, market testing provides a wealth of data for marketing decisions, particularly for pricing decisions and decisions related to sales forecasts. If you have some idea of your customers' price sensitivity, you can predict the effect of various prices, and price changes, on their buying behavior. That helps you set the price of the new product. Sales forecasts serve as the basis for production forecasts, which drive decisions about labor, materials, storage, and transportation resources.

Unfortunately, rigorous market testing, which incorporates statistically significant samples, just isn't practical for many products. If you have a new, complex, expensive industrial product or computer system or specialized scanning equipment for hospitals, you cannot really segment test participants and test buying behavior as you would for a new breakfast cereal.

Still, knowing the principles of sound market testing can only help an innovator. That's because those principles include developing a research plan, defining ways of measuring customer behavior, gathering and analyzing data on that behavior, and drawing useful conclusions on the basis of that data. This kind of procedure produces solid information for any decision.

Here are hints for testing the two key

aspects of buying behavior—purchase volume and price sensitivity.

Purchase Volume

Purchase volume includes the amount purchased and the frequency of purchases. If these are a consideration for your product, you'll need to hold a market test that's long enough to gauge these factors, which may mean testing over a few months. It's not really an issue for many B-to-B products, such as computer systems, nor is it for major consumer purchases, such as kitchen appliances, because of the product's long life.

However, for consumer packaged goods, for anything that comes as part of a set, (such as Beanie Babies), and for anything that can be upgraded with extra attachments, service contracts, and so on, the amount purchased is worth measuring.

Key questions to answer when analyzing data on purchase amount and frequency include:

- *How do amount and frequency vary among various types of customers?*

- *What are the characteristics of heavy, medium, and light users?*

- *How do these various buyers use the product?*

- *When does purchase volume or frequency rise and fall?*

- *What are the implications for our sales forecast?*

Price Sensitivity

Price sensitivity measures the relationship between price and purchase volume for a product. The relationship is usually stated in this way: For every X percent decrease (or increase) in price, sales volume increases (or decreases) by Y percent. Analyzing price sensitivity helps a company set the price of a product at the level that will maximize sales and profits.

Basic pricing theory states that the lower the price, the more people will purchase; the higher the price, the less people will purchase. There are, however, interesting exceptions to this such as Scotch and designer luggage, where higher prices create the perception of value. This also often occurs with personal and professional services.

To obtain a valid measure of price sensitivity, the market test must be designed to test for it. This means carefully selecting the samples and controlling other, nonprice factors that might affect buying behavior, such as the availability of the product, or competitors' price changes. It also means gathering the right data and properly analyzing the results. These tasks usually call for an expert in statistical analysis. It's important to do whatever you can to find a price that maximizes your profits.

" EARLY TO BED, EARLY TO RISE, **WORK LIKE HELL,** AND ADVERTISE. "

—Ted Turner
(founder, CNN and
Turner Broadcasting
System)

Rolling Out New Products and Services

8

At this point, your innovation has been invented, developed, designed, and tested. You have your production facility or a contract with a reliable producer. If you're in a service business, you have the resources to deliver the services in place. Now all you have to do is locate customers, make them aware of your innovation, and convince them to buy it. In other words, here comes the hard part—the product launch.

In this chapter we examine the elements of a successful product or service launch. A launch, also known as a rollout, represents an

pro•duct launch

1. introduction of a new or improved product to new customers
2. phase of a marketing campaign designed to win the Early Adopters
3. also known as a rollout, from automotive and airplane manufacturers, which roll the new models off the assembly line or out of hangars

THE FIVE Ps OF MARKETING

- **Product:** Your product or service must meet the customers' needs.

- **Price:** The price must be right for the customer and the company.

- **Packaging:** You need functional and attractive packaging.

- **Place:** To sell something, you have to get it in front of customers.

- **Promotion:** You must get out the word about the product.

intensive marketing effort focused tightly on getting word of the product out and getting people to buy it. That, of course, is what most of marketing consists of, but the newness of the product makes the launch a particularly challenging marketing task.

Three Keys to a Successful Launch

You must deal with the Five Ps of Marketing—product, price, packaging, place, and promotion—whenever you prepare any marketing effort. For a launch, however, I think in terms of Three Ms—markets, messages, and media. You must launch the product to the right markets with the right messages through the right media. Let's look at ways to identify the right ones.

The Right Markets: Innovators and Early Adopters

The right markets for a new product are the people or organizations who'll be most willing to buy it—the Innovators and Early Adopters. (Again, I'll use "product" to mean product or service.) Targeting these market segments precisely is less important when rolling out a low-priced, mass-market item. Colgate-Palmolive doesn't have to hunt down the first 2.5 percent of the population who will buy a new tooth whitening product. They can place it in stores, advertise and promote it, and the first consumers to buy it will, by definition, be the Innovators.

When you are selling a specialized B-to-B product, rather than a commodity, targeting becomes more important, and more difficult. Launching high-tech products, industrial equipment, and items sold through architects, contractors, or designers also calls for identifying the most likely prospects among those who will ultimately buy the product. Even certain mass-market products, such as pricey fragrances and shampoos, benefit when you identify the early buyers and target them, say, through the magazines they read.

There are several ways of identifying early buyers, depending on whether you are selling a consumer product or a B-to-B product, so let's examine consumer and B-to-B methods separately.

I'll-Try-It Consumers

The usual demographic and psychographic characteristics for consumers may or may not be useful identifiers of Innovators and Early Adopters for your product or service. For example, traditional markers such as income or social class work well for automobiles and alcoholic beverages, but offer fewer guideposts for certain products, such as consumer electronics, computing products, Internet services, and power tools. Someone who's conservative about purchasing new car models may go wild for the latest software.

How Do You Find the First Buyers?

If you already have customers, consider those who have tried new products or features in the past. Also, consider customers who have asked for improvements. Review your records from the concept, product, and market tests, and look for those customers who seemed most interested in the product. Heavy users of a product category are often the first to try new products in that category. For instance, seasoned travelers would be more interested in exotic locales than would people who've never left their continents.

Try to identify the relevant characteristics of those people. What's their age and their income range? Where do they live, in terms of geography and type of dwelling? What are their other interests?

de•mo•graph•ic and psy•cho•graph•ic char•ac•ter•is•tics

1. demographic factors include gender, age, income, education, marital status, ethnic background, education, and number of children
2. psychographic factors include lifestyle, social class, personality traits, status consciousness, environmental consciousness, and political leanings

Early B-to-B Buyers

For most B-to-B products, early buyers should be easier to identify. They want to make or save money with the purchase, so look for outfits with operations that would benefit the most from what you sell. Indeed, if you know your customers and the concept, product, and market test results, you'll have a good idea of those most likely to try the new offering.

If you're an innovator, you should know who the most forward-thinking, aggressive, competitive companies—and even individuals—are among the potential customers in your product or service category. They tend to be either rapidly growing companies or established ones with excellent track records and reputations.

If you're a start-up and don't have any customers, look at the most innovative customers of your competitors. If you're in a new product category, be careful here. Skiers didn't constitute the market for snowboards; surfers and skateboarders did. Indeed, most skiers looked down on snowboarding for years, and many still do. However, surfers and skateboarders were younger and more likely to try new things (and, of course, wanted a winter substitute for their warm-weather sports).

Finally, note which participants in the concept, market, and product tests seemed most forward-thinking and genuinely interested in your new product. Even if they don't buy, they may point you to companies with a similar profile.

The Right Messages: Novelty and Value

The specific marketing message depends on the product and its price, performance, and complexity. However, the right message will always (a) capture and hold the prospect's attention, and (b) communicate a powerful value proposition.

To capture attention for a consumer product launch, tout the novelty and anything exotic about the product. Those advertisers who say "Be the first on your block to try it" know that being the first appeals to Innovators. So does anything exotic. They like to see themselves, and to be seen by others, as adventurous and sophisticated.

Be sure to convey a benefit—and its value—as soon as you can. Particularly in a B-to-B launch, stress the competitive advantages and superior performance that the new product or service will provide. Innovators and Early Adopters find

---

val•ue prop•o•si•tion

1. reason a customer should purchase a product or service
2. distinguishing or unique benefit of the product or service
3. also known as unique selling proposition, or USP

---

messages about competitive advantages and high performance compelling. Phrases such as "for the first time," "at last," "market leaders see the difference," and "forty percent more power" get their attention.

> Customers will step along the path to the sale only if you communicate what's-in-it-for-them at every step.
>
> —**Mike Webb (founder, Sales Performance Consultants, Inc.)**

Copy Strategies

After you have their attention, you must clarify and reinforce the value proposition. Such messages take skill and effort to craft.

Find ways of differentiating the product that your customers will find compelling. Then build a message around that. Here are five basic copy strategies and the related value proposition:

> **cop•y strat•e•gy**
>
> 1. approach for engaging the customer in an advertisement or sales message
> 2. also known as message design

    1. Cite a problem that your competitors have, but you don't: Finally, a group health-care plan that really reduces your costs! (Value proposition: You'll save money with our new plan.)

    2. Play off an existing trend or controversy: Is your company in compliance with all new federal rules and regulations? (Value proposition: You'll stay out of court and out of jail.)

3. Cite a major improvement customers will experience: Increase your customer traffic by 20 percent within ninety days! (Value proposition: You'll bring more customers into your store.)

4. Reduce the risk of trying something new: Our new FlowMeter saves you 20 percent off your fuel bills—or we pay you double the difference! (Value proposition: You can't lose!)

5. Cite the problem you've solved: Here's a data management system that marketing and accounting can agree on! (Value proposition: You'll reduce internal conflict and confusion.)

Memorable Sales Messages

Sometimes the memorable message reflects an actual product characteristic. Altoids mints are "curiously strong" and British. Coors beer is made with Rocky Mountain water. Other characteristics are created: Absolut vodka characterized itself as hip by visual association with certain people (Warhol) and places (Napa Valley, LA), and even the changes in seasons, the latter making it seem always up-to-date.

To write good advertising and sales copy, you must deeply understand the product, its benefits, and why and how people use it, including their psychological motivations. Good copywriters find something unique and interesting about the product—how it was developed, where it's made, which ingredient makes a difference—and tie it to something the customer wants, such as dependability and long life, ease of use, or adventure, status, security, or refreshment.

Sales Challenges

Some people think of a product launch as occurring on a grand scale. That may be so for low-price, mass-market products, such as foods and consumer packaged goods. But with high-ticket, complex products and services in both consumer and B-to-B markets, you need face-to-face selling. You need salespeople to overcome serious sales challenges, and to work with customers to learn their needs, address their concerns, overcome their objections, and close the deal.

In B-to-B markets, the major sales challenges are risk, complexity, total cost (which includes the cost of changes customers must make to use the product), and entrenched competition. In consumer markets, the major sales challenges are lack of awareness, lack of perceived need, risk, cost, and often, complexity.

Salespeople help customers understand the product. They answer customers' questions—provided you've equipped them with solid sales materials and, if necessary, training via video media or even in person, and with demonstration models. Make your launch material easy to read and use. Consider establishing a hot line where salespeople can get questions answered. Some companies "seed" the marketplace by giving the new product free to salespeople. This works with cell phones and other fun-to-use, high-tech products, where an on-the-spot recommendation can close the sale.

Working with Outside Sales Channels

Many companies rely on wholesalers, retailers, distributors, dealers, and other sales channels to sell new products. In those cases, the launch must target two audiences—the consumers (or end users), and the sales channels (also known as channel partners).

You must detail features and benefits to your channel partners, but then there's more to do. You must point out the likely sales challenges and objections they'll face, and help them identify likely customers by profile or by name. Also, consider the profit your channel partners will realize on your product versus alternatives they can sell. Usually, channel partners sell what they make the most

sales chan•nels

1. retailers, wholesalers, distributors, OEMs (original equipment manufacturers), and other "middlemen" who help bring a product to customers
2. means of distribution that lies outside the company
3. also known as channel partners

money on or what they can most easily sell. Try to play to one of those motivations when you deal with channel partners.

Give sales partners temporary bonuses on new products, and then phase out the bonuses after the product is established. The sales partners won't like that, but it's easier than actually cutting their profits later.

Sales Channel Strategies

A new car stereo system company recruited every car stereo dealer in the phone book, plus a major retail chain, and soon found itself doing too much for too few sales. An analysis revealed that certain dealers were by far their best producers, and the retail chain, being less sophisticated, used too much support time. The company focused its resources on the best dealers to take share from competitors, and dropped the chain.

Note too that when it comes to stimulating demand for a new product to be sold through channel partners, you face a chicken-and-egg situation (or is it the other way around?). In some situations stores won't stock an item until customers ask for it, and customers won't ask for it until they see it displayed in the stores. In these situations you have to target marketing efforts to the dealers and the customers, perhaps on a smaller scale or in a more limited geographical area than you would prefer, or you must work harder to get dealers excited about the product, so they will make customers aware of it.

The Right Media: Use a Mix

Regardless of your product, service, market, customers, or company size, you must carefully choose the media and materials for delivering your messages to your markets. In most product launches, it's best to use a mix of elements, for several reasons: Using various media enables you to repeat the message, but with a different spin. Also, different media and materials serve different purposes, and some people respond more readily to certain tactics than to others.

Broadly, here's the menu of marketing media and materials, and what they do:

- *Sales kits and product literature include marketing material (or "collateral") such as brochures, diagrams, case studies and success stories, lists of satisfied customers, and charts of money saved by using the product.*

- *Demonstrations and free samples bring the product to life for customers and show them how easy it is to use, how great it tastes, and so on.*

- *Promotion generally means tools for grabbing attention—especially in retail stores—and purchase incentives such as coupons, special offers,* two-fors, and items such as tote bags, umbrellas, and mugs. Product placements and celebrity endorsements fall into this category, too.

Watch Big Pharma

Major pharmaceutical companies use the full menu of media in rollouts. They advertise to consumers on TV and in magazines. They advertise to physicians in trade magazines. Their Web sites include information for patients and physicians. To see how well they use the Web, browse the sites for Propecia (Merck), Claritin (Schering-Plough), and Nexium (AstraZeneca).

○ Guarantees, warranties, and service contracts belong in the mix if your customers' concerns include maintenance and dependability—risks associated with purchasing almost any new product.

○ Trade shows and conferences give you "face time" with potential customers, and enable you to announce a new product with a splash, but watch your costs and learn beforehand what competitors may be announcing.

○ Advertising includes any messages that you pay to have carried in print, broadcast, cable, satellite, outdoor, wireless, or Web-based media.

○ Public relations (or PR) includes coverage, such as stories about your product or interviews with users, that you obtain in any medium without paying the medium, although you *may pay a public relations agency to help you get the coverage.*

○ *Web-based tactics include most of those I've mentioned above, plus a few others that I'll discuss below.*

○ *Word of mouth is the most powerful "media" of all, but it's hard to control. However, that has not stopped some outfits from trying.*

To choose wisely from this menu, you must decide which materials and media will work best for your product and markets. In overall marketing efforts and in product launches, many companies are migrating away from advertising and toward public relations, Web-based efforts, and more personal forms of marketing, such as buzz marketing. Let's examine these three tools, because they are becoming increasingly important in product launches.

The Rise of Public Relations

Public relations has become far more important than it had been, relative to advertising, over the past ten years or so. Public relations includes any media coverage or "mentions" for which you do not pay the publication or broadcaster, although you may pay a public relations firm to help you get that coverage. PR consists of articles that you or people in your company write for magazines, newspapers, newsletters, and other publications; articles in which a journalist writes about your company or product; radio or television interviews; and speeches at events and conferences, when those are covered by the media.

PR has always had the advantage of credibility over advertising. Many people reason that if a journalist or a producer covers something as news then it must be newsworthy and true—and it may well be.

However, we all know that if *Time* magazine runs a cover story on a movie released by Warner Brothers, it might have something to do with the fact that Time Warner owns both companies. We also know that when major companies hire major PR firms to help them gain coverage, they typically get it. Was the product or company really newsworthy? Or does the PR firm have relationships with the media that help them get that coverage?

Target media consciously and with an eye toward what the early buyers of your product are likely to read, watch, listen to, and browse. Everyone wants "ink" in the New York Times and, for business products, the *Wall Street Journal, BusinessWeek*, and *Fortune*. That's why those publications receive hundreds of press releases and story ideas every day. Yet in any market segment, people read trade and

press re•lease

1. one- to two-page write-up in a standard format announcing a newsworthy product, event, or change
2. basic public relations tool, distributed to selected media electronically, by fax, or, less often, by mail

special-interest magazines and newsletters, and browse specialized Web sites. This is especially true of Innovators and Early Adopters, because they focus intensely on their interests. Bear in mind that just a mention in an article or broadcast can be valuable.

Webbed Launches

Today, every product launch must be supported by a Web strategy. This goes beyond putting up a Web site and taking the rest of the day off. It also entails:

Take Action
See www.press-release-writing.com *for basic information and tips on writing press releases.*

- Pointing people to your Web site in all of your marketing materials and in any advertisements you use

- Establishing relationships and building trust with visitors to the site

- Offering information or diagnostic tools in exchange for contact data

- Staying in touch with people who register interest in your site through occasional newsletters, announcements, and promotions

- Making your product or service available through a Web-based ordering and payment mechanism, if possible

Consider linking with other sites, and perhaps establishing other information-only sites or affiliate group sites to extend your presence in cyberspace. Also, if you plan to seriously use the Web as a marketing medium, you should understand search engine optimization (SEO) methods that will help your site rank high in the results of searches related to your business and products.

Word of Mouth: The Ultimate Medium

Positive word of mouth may be the single most powerful promotional tool, especially for new products. That's proven every time a movie is released; no matter how big the stars or the advertising budget, if people hate the flick, they tell their friends and it dies. Conversely, many movies with no stars and small budgets succeed on word of mouth.

The technology adoption curve implies that people talk and listen to one another, so do all that you can to ensure that you get good buzz marketing. You have to have a great product or service, treat customers well, and quickly fix anything that goes wrong. People understand that mistakes happen, and customers can be understanding if the product is new. But they can't understand why a company doesn't fix something that goes wrong. When they feel that a company has treated them badly, they tell people about it.

Buzz Marketing

Finally, a word about buzz marketing, which is also known as viral marketing because it aims to spread the word like a virus, from person to person, until there's an epidemic. Buzz marketers plant people in the population they want to influence. These people typically seem, at least at first, to be unconnected to the product. Buzz marketers do this at nightclubs, on beaches, in malls, on blogs, and in chatrooms. These planted people talk up the product, tell people where to buy it, and so on.

It's an effective form of marketing—at least for now—for new products. As with any other form of marketing, its effectiveness will diminish with overuse. Also, word of mouth runs the risk of commercializing our daily interactions without our realizing it. When an acquaintance at my health club raves about a new shampoo or nutrition bar, I'd like to know that he's not being paid to do it.

Take Action

To understand viral marketing and "social epidemics," read Malcolm Gladwell's The Tipping Point *(Little, Brown, 2000) It's one of those rare books that introduced a new term into everyday conversation.*

The Product Launch Plan

All the elements come together in a product launch plan. This plan includes a timeline and schedule of goals, steps required to achieve each goal, and tasks necessary to execute each step. Broadly, the plan would call for:

○ *Identifying the target markets, and perhaps even target customers, for your new product; for most non-mass-*

market products, this means locating the Innovators and Early Adopters

- Developing marketing and sales messages for these target markets, and adapting them to the materials and media you intend to use

- Creating marketing materials, sales literature, advertisements, samples, promotional displays, and a Web site

- Deciding which sales channels you will use—salespeople, direct mail, distributors, and so on—and preparing them to sell

- Understanding what it will take to deliver the product, get customers started, and resolve problems, and putting those resources in place

- Defining a timeframe for preparing and deploying your marketing and sales messages in the various media

- Implementing the plan according to schedule, while allowing for the inevitable glitches and setbacks

In the process, you must identify and line up the resources you'll need, such as a Web design firm, advertising agency, distributor, and, of course, the funds to pay for these resources.

Launch, Then Grow

Remember, the launch stage aims primarily to sell to the Innovators and Early Adopters. After they're on board, you must shift into the growth stage, and your messages and media may have to change. As you make these changes, try not to abandon your earlier customers; instead, bring them along by continuing to meet their needs.

INNOVATION IN
SPECIFIC SITUATIONS

part

3

" OUR **SUCCESS** HAS REALLY BEEN
BASED ON PARTNERSHIPS
FROM THE VERY BEGINNING. **"**

—Bill Gates
(founder, Microsoft)

Making Money from Innovations

To make money from an innovation, you have to put it to work and exploit it fully. I use the word "exploit" here in the sense of using something to make money. Exploiting an innovation means developing, testing, and launching it. You don't have to do all those things by yourself, though. Today, there are more ways than ever to get those things done and to make money from an innovation—even if it's someone else's, as long as you obtain the legal right to use it.

My aim here is to explain the main ways in which you can get an innovation developed, produced, and sold, even if you don't work for a large organization or don't plan to start an actual operating business. Chapter 11 will discuss starting up a business based on an innovation; this chapter focuses on working with other businesses.

About Strategic Alliances

"Strategic alliance" is the general term for agreements, partnerships, and ventures between two businesses or companies. For the purposes of this chapter, consider yourself a business unless you own a company or work for one. You can form strategic alliances on your own, but will usually have more leverage in negotiations if you have a business or at least a business identity.

stra•te•gic al•li•ance

1. formal agreement between two companies to work in a defined area for mutual benefit
2. umbrella term for arrangements in which two (or more) businesses join forces to develop a product or market

Companies form strategic alliances for various reasons. In general, one company owns or has access to a technology, product, market, sales channel, or methodology that the other company can benefit from. For example, a company that makes security systems may form alliances with companies that build homes or office buildings, or with car or boat manufacturers or dealers. The security systems company gets access to those markets, and the builder or manufacturer has an attractive feature to offer customers. In any well-structured, well-managed strategic alliance, both companies benefit in very direct ways.

We'll return to the motives for forming strategic alliances, and look at what constitutes a well-structured and well-managed alliance as well. First, however, let's examine the various types of alliances.

Watch Your Assets

Strategic alliances are fraught with legal issues, and I am not providing legal advice. Rather, I am explaining ways of exploiting innovations from the businessperson's perspective. Before you approach any party or enter into any kind of business agreement or contract, obtain competent legal advice and a legal review of the documents.

Buddy Up: Types of Strategic Alliances

The most common types of strategic alliances include:

- *Distribution and marketing arrangements—In these agreements, Company A has a product that Company B could sell to its customers. So they agree that Company B will sell Company A's product, either alone or bundled with one or more of its products.*

- *Comarketing and copromotion arrangements—These are marketing arrangements driven by the compatibility or complementary nature of companies' products. For example, when Disney, Mattel, and McDonald's team up to sell Happy Meals with figurines of characters from the Disney movie, that's comarketing and copromotion.*

- Joint research or codevelopment agreements—Company A and Company B each have part of a product, formulation, or system, and can create the whole thing more effectively or efficiently by working together. Another possibility is that a large company wants to tap a smaller company's creativity. Major pharmaceutical companies have been partnering with small biotech firms in these arrangements for years.

- Licensing agreements—These are marketing, development, or research agreements in which Company A (the licenser) confers certain rights to use its innovation, material, or brand to Company B (the licensee), for a fee, royalty, or both. Royalties are payments based on sales of products marketed under the licensed brand.

- OEM (original equipment manufacturer) arrangements—Company B uses Company A's innovation, components, or parts in manufacturing its products or systems. Most local or regional computer and networking companies are OEMs who use generic components to build computers and networks for their customers, to whom they then provide service and support.

- Joint ventures—This term is often used loosely, but a true joint venture is a separate entity, such as a business or R & D facility, created by Company A and Company B to develop an *innovation or market or to exploit a particular opportunity.*

○ *Other arrangements—these include various types of partnerships and options, as well as forms of equity participation, in which Company A invests in Company B, thus providing funding in return for an ownership stake.*

Businesses and individuals can enter into contracts for any legal purpose. This means that the ways in which business partners can agree to work together are limited only by economic realities and their imaginations.

In practice the types of strategic alliances overlap, and the lines that define them can blur. For example, when Dell uses Intel chips in its computers, is it an OEM agreement, a comarketing or copromotion agreement, or a licensing agreement? Actually, it has features of all three. Dell is essentially an OEM that builds computers to order, promotes "Intel Inside," and is licensed to use Intel's brand on its products. An agreement's actual terms are more important than the terminology.

Strategic alliances are sometimes unions of equals in size and financial and marketing strength, but that is not usually

> **OEM**
> 1. original equipment manufacturer
> 2. company that constructs computers, systems, or other products from components supplied by other companies
> 3. companies with assembly expertise combined with strong branding and marketing

the case. Major companies, such as IBM, Microsoft, Hewlett-Packard, Xerox, Corning, Disney, and all of the major pharmaceutical companies, use strategic alliances all the time. Generally, however, they form them with smaller companies (or with large companies that have complementary goals and resources).

I am not suggesting that you approach *Fortune* 500 companies with the goal of forming a strategic alliance, although I wouldn't presume to discourage you. Instead, I am suggesting that you research, locate, evaluate, and approach businesses or individuals who might make suitable strategic partners—if such a partner would help you toward your goals. The businesses you approach may be small compared to a corporate giant, but if they help you make or market your innovation, then their size is immaterial. If they can make use of your innovation or bring it to market in ways that profit you, then you may well have a basis for doing business with one another.

Unless you have an extremely attractive technology or product, you may find it hard to get the attention of an executive at a major company. In all likelihood, the value you can add to a smaller strategic partner would probably be greater to that partner than to a corporate giant.

To propose an alliance with a major company, have a business plan for the

Take Action

Visit the Web sites www .alliancestrategy.com, www.strategic-alliances .org, *and* www.alliance analyst.com *for more information about strategic alliances.*

innovation (see Chapter 12) and an idea of what you can offer and what you want from the company. Then search the Web and network at the company to locate the executive in charge of evaluating alliances and external business opportunities.

The Right Relationships

While the goals, responsibilities, rewards, and conditions in an alliance should be clear, no contract can make a bad relationship work. Therefore, focus on the relationship as well as on the deal. It's easy to focus on the deal, on who gets what and who contributes what, but it's actually the relationship between the parties that will make or break the alliance. A spirit of collaboration, and not just cooperation, characterizes solid alliances.

In some cases, the parties feel so good about one another that they neglect business details. Ultimately a business relationship will always be about business, which means who is doing what for how much money.

Much comes down to setting and managing expectations. One of the reasons to craft a detailed agreement is for the parties to get to know one another and to develop a sense of shared expectations. If Company A continually expects something that Company B wants to withhold, or vice versa, a good working alliance may be impossible. If that's the case, it's best to know that beforehand.

What Can Go Wrong?

Aside from those covered or implied so far, certain mistakes are easy to make when forming strategic alliances. Here are five things not to do:

1. Don't expect synergy. Synergy occurs when the whole is greater than the sum of its parts. Synergy in business partnerships is not the buzzword it once was, because it's proven so elusive. Indeed, the supposedly synergistic merger of Time Warner with America Online (AOL) actually gave synergy a bad name. When synergy occurs, it's almost always apparent only after the fact, and therefore not to be expected.

2. Don't count on ancillary benefits. Ancillary benefits are like synergy. They are hoped-for positive side effects rather than things you can actively pursue. The trouble is, they're often used to justify the deal. For instance, you may be an innovator who hopes that getting involved with a large company will automatically lead to good things.

3. Don't duplicate weaknesses—or strengths. It's easy to join forces with someone in the same situation that you're in, but it usually won't help either of you. Most successful alliances are founded on complementary—and not duplicate—capabilities or problems.

4. Don't expect the alliance to manage itself. Large companies that form many alliances usually have alliance managers who keep them on track. Often two businesses will form an alliance and expect subordinates to then "make it happen." This rarely works. There's nothing magical about a strategic alliance. Instead, it's a lot of work.

5. Don't spread yourself too thin. Some large companies view strategic alliances as a numbers game. This can be like dating six people at the same time and wondering why none of the relationships worked out. That said, an alliance strategy based on a well-managed portfolio of partnerships can work for a large company. However, the smaller company can wind up like one of the six people being dated. If you partner with a larger company, get a sense of where you stand in the scheme of things, what else the company is working on in your area, and what it expects to achieve in a given timeframe.

There are stories of companies that have purchased innovations simply to take them off the market and eliminate a potential competitor. These stories are almost impossible to verify because companies don't admit to such things, and innovators can be mistaken. Yet, stranger things have happened.

STEPS IN SECURING AN ALLIANCE

- Define your criteria

- Search for potential partners

- Devise an approach

- Make contact and start talking

How to Go About It

There are decisions you must make and questions you must answer before you seek and secure a strategic alliance. Among them are these:

- Decide what the innovation needs. What will make the innovation complete and attractive? What will it take to make it properly and price it attractively? How should it be marketed and distributed to various customers? Which organizations or people can help you do these things?

- Decide what you need. What do you require in terms of rewards? What tasks are you willing and able to handle? What risks can you assume? What time and other resources can you contribute?

Take Action
To start learning about contract manufacturers, check out online directories such as www.thomasnet.com and www.b2bchinasources .com.

Get It Made

In Chapter 7, I mentioned that you can take your design and product specifications to a contract manufacturer and have that company produce your product. The complexity involved in finding and working with a contract manufacturer depends on the complexity of your innovation. If it's a tote bag, you face a relatively simple task. If it's a heart rate monitor, you face a more complex one.

In any event, engaging a contract manufacturer represents a potentially large financial outlay, so be sure to obtain guidance from an experienced consultant or entrepreneur. You must consider factors such as the reputation and reliability of the manufacturer, as well as production, shipping, and storage costs. Research several manufacturers and talk to entrepreneurs who have used them. If your innovation requires significant labor, consider working with a manufacturer in Mexico or Asia.

Request bids from several manufacturers and freight companies, and ask why their prices are what they are; in the end, the lowest bid is not always the least expensive. Never enter any agreement without full knowledge of all dimensions of the deal and competent legal advice, especially when doing business overseas. Many innovators have paid a lot of money to have thousands of items produced, only to find that the products are not salable because basic procedures were neglected.

Take Action
Read The Wisdom of Ginsu *(Career Press, 2005) by Barry Becher and Edward Valenti, the guys who made millions (and made millions laugh) marketing the Ginsu Knife on television.*

"WHEN YOU TRY TO FORMALIZE OR SOCIALIZE **CREATIVE ACTIVITY,** THE ONLY SURE RESULT IS COMMERCIAL CONSTIPATION."

—Charles Browder
(advertising executive)

Managing Corporate Innovation

10

As I noted in Chapter 3, some large companies cannot innovate, although many others can. In this chapter, we'll look at problems in corporate innovation and at the ways in which successful companies overcome them.

Companies that resist innovation do so because innovation means change. Large, successful companies got that way by doing certain things in certain ways, and if they innovate, they must abandon, to some degree, the things that made them successful. Of course, innovating made many of those companies successful in the first place. So why don't they keep innovating? What problems do they face when they do try to innovate?

Six Problems in Corporate Innovation

Much of the research on why large companies don't innovate explains what people working in large outfits see every day. It's usually not so much that innovations fail, but rather that the companies fail even to try to innovate.

Failure to Identify Customers' Needs

Customers' real needs revolve around what they want to accomplish, both in the buying process and with the product or service. It's amazing how long it can take an industry to respond to customers' needs. For instance, when people started using Amazon.com, wouldn't the needs being filled be clear to anyone? Brick-and-mortar bookstores are wonderful places, but customers need wide selection, ready access to titles, and reviews and opinions.

Online bookstores fill those needs better than traditional bookstores. The question is, why didn't traditional bookstores try to meet those needs before Amazon came along—for instance, by developing faster ordering and shipping methods and making more reviews available? Why do they keep their ordering systems behind the counter? Why didn't they arrange to ship books to customers' homes instead of making them come into the store to pick them up?

Not Invented Here

A kind of arrogance and even snobbery characterizes many corporate cultures, and it contributes to what's known as the not-invented-here syndrome. Companies with this outlook won't purchase new technologies or adopt new methods mainly because they did not develop them (they were "not invented here" at our company).

This attitude led technologists in many IT departments to expend their companies' resources developing their own software systems for functions such as accounting, when off-the-shelf packages would have been equally good, or at least good enough. It also leads companies to develop and make components and materials themselves when they could easily purchase them from other companies.

This is not, however, as big a problem as it used to be. Cost pressures and an awareness that you can work with suppliers to get what you need has made not-invented-here less prevalent, but it still can be found.

Short-Term Focus

Observers of business, and many managers, have for decades decried the lack of long-term thinking among senior executives. It's a real problem, and it's exacerbated by the current system of executive compensation, which is tied to annual earnings and stock prices. Many investors also focus on short-term gains.

When executives and investors seek the maximum in short-term financial performance, companies give innovation and other long-term efforts low priority. Innovation does direct resources into efforts that probably won't pay off in the near term, but when managed properly they do pay off in the longer term, and often handsomely.

Maximizing short-term earnings leads management to cut costs in order to boost earnings. While minimizing costs generally makes sense, it won't generate long-term earnings growth. Only investment can do that. That means investment in productive capacity, market development, and innovation.

Not Knowing What They Have

Occasionally a company will develop a new technology and either choose not to develop an application from it or fail to understand how to make money with it. Probably the most famous case of this is the point-and-click GUI (graphical user interface, pronounced "gooey") technology developed by Xerox Palo Alto Research Center (PARC), Xerox's research and development facility.

Xerox developed this and other personal computer technologies and did indeed apply them in a product. However, it was Apple's Macintosh, based on that same GUI technology, that was the first commercially successful product of this type.

Failure to Recognize Threats and Decline

Not only are some companies too wedded to current products and markets, but they also

Take Action
Visit www.parc.xerox.com *for more information on Xerox PARC.*

often fail to see marketplace threats and signs of aging products. Threats include new competitors, especially those with technologies that could supersede yours. Signs of aging products include flat or declining sales or profits, which signal the maturity or decline phases of the life cycle.

Also watch for market saturation. Closely monitor the yields on direct mail, Web-based, or in-person sales efforts. When those yields decrease, it could be that your company only needs to improve those efforts—or it could be that the market is getting saturated. There's very little that sales efforts can do about market saturation.

The answer to almost all threats of this type is to exit the business, sell the product line, become the low-cost provider, or innovate. The strategies suggested for the maturity and decline phases in Chapter 2 may be useful, but if you face a disruptive technology, an overwhelming competitor, or a saturated market, you have limited options. Watch for red flags that signal these developments.

There is nothing wrong with discontinuing a product line. Many companies let a dying product languish too long before putting it out of its misery.

mar•ket sat•u•ra•tion

1. every customer who might use the product or service has purchased it
2. point at which the market for a product or service stops growing
3. maturity phase for a product or class of products

Oddly, some companies see trouble coming but don't innovate. Instead, they just "try harder" by increasing marketing and sales efforts, or they cut prices. These can be good short-term responses, but if a product or service is in decline, the path forward is to innovate.

Corporate Bureaucracy

Large organizations generate bureaucracy, which stifles innovation. Large size isolates companies from customers. Everything takes longer because more managers must approve decisions. More people in the company, as well as customers and suppliers, have vested interests in current products and operations.

It's often said that a large organization resembles an ocean liner—it takes time to turn it around. That's true, but several things can help. We examine those things in the remainder of this chapter.

How Successful Companies Innovate

As I noted in Chapter 3, senior executives know that large companies often find innovation difficult. Executives and consultants have, however, developed ways to deal with these difficulties. Some are general guidelines; others are specific tactics.

RED FLAGS

○ *Declining sales or profits*

○ *Repetitive complaints or legal threats*

○ *Customer defections*

○ *Substitute products*

Before we look at specific tactics, here are a few general requirements for corporate innovation:

- *Strong management commitment. The things that get done in a company are the things senior management wants done. Without strong senior level support, innovation will not be taken seriously, and the budget will be cut whenever money gets tight.*

- *Skilled people. R & D and product development must be staffed with innovators and with managers who can oversee them. You can't assign people to innovation for political reasons. They require the right education, knowledge, experience, temperament, and skills.*

- *Proper investment. Investing too much can be as bad as underfunding innovation. A good argument can be made for slight underfunding, because people may become more creative and work harder to produce results. However, committing way too few resources will undercut the effort and cause good people to leave for places that take innovation seriously.*

- *Mechanisms for disseminating innovations. Every large company needs ways to tell the various divisions in the corporation about the technologies and methods that have been developed elsewhere in the organization. That way, the divisions can apply them to customers' needs in new products*

MEASURES OF SUCCESSFUL INNOVATION

- *Number of new products*

- *Revenue/profits from new products*

- *New product success ratio*

- *Number of patents granted*

- *Return on investment in innovation*

and services. Every company also needs someone working on licensing or selling innovations to other organizations.

○ Clear processes, goals, and measurements. Innovation requires a defined process so that managers know what skills and resources are necessary, what progress is or isn't being made, and where adjustments may be needed. Any process requires interim and ultimate goals, so that management can measure progress. The company must also know what it spends and earns on innovation efforts.

Without these or at least most of these conditions in place, most specific tactics will be doomed to failure. That said, specific tactics include:

○ Having an innovation game plan

○ Using dedicated development units

○ Scanning and searching the marketplace

○ Promoting technology transfer

○ Reducing time to market

Have an Innovation Game Plan

Virtually every company needs a game plan for using technology and applications to fuel growth by means of new products and services. A true game plan takes four key factors into account: customer needs; current products; technologies and applications to develop, find, and use; and competitive, regulatory, and other marketplace developments.

Leaving out any one of these exposes a company to real danger. Aging products are one common example. If a company isn't developing new technologies, applications, and products, it is almost certain to decline, because all products eventually decline. In service industries, a new competitor using technology to deliver faster, better, cheaper service may be just around the corner. Note that a company doesn't have to develop its own technologies or even its own applications, but it must develop new products and improved services in order to remain vital.

Carefully monitoring products' life cycles enables a company to phase out and introduce products in an orderly manner, rather than reactively. Products must serve customer needs, but you can't become imprisoned by your customers' agendas. If you do, you'll be blind-sided by competitors' new technologies—which your customers will eagerly adopt.

Always know your customers' posture toward innovations. Are you selling to Innovators and Early Adopters, or to the Late Majority and Laggards? Do you have products for customers in various segments of the technology adoption curve, or do you sell to only one or two of those segments? In either case, what lies ahead, given your portfolio of products? The correct answers to these questions depend on the company and its strategy and resources, but not answering them leaves you reacting to marketplace developments rather than being prepared or leading the way.

Finally, not every company can, should, or needs to be an innovator. The value of first-mover advantage is widely debated. Often, the first mover incurs huge costs to develop the product and the market, only to fail. Failure can stem from running out of money or facing competitors who have more resources and the benefit of the pioneer's experience, as did Google in outdoing other search engines, such as AskJeeves.

Business people who don't think that being the first mover is worthwhile often point out that typically, it is the pioneers in a new land who get killed.

---

first-mov•er ad•van•tage

1. market position and extraordinary sales and profits that can result from being the first company to introduce a technology or product 2. subject of debate because the benefits might not outweigh the costs

---

Use Dedicated Development Units

Companies that live and die by the strength of their research and development functions, such as pharmaceutical companies and innovators in industries including chemicals, instruments, electronics, and optics, have dedicated R & D units. These are staffed by scientists working in basic research (bench scientists), as well as product developers. For instance, in a pharmaceutical company, research chemists work on the relationship between chemistry and disease processes. The application will become a new medication or class of medications. The product will be the dosage, form (such as liquid, capsule, or tablet), benefits, and brand.

Product developers work at formulating products rather than basic science. For instance, a food packager might not work on artificial sweeteners, but rather purchase them, test them in its kitchens, and formulate products that include them.

In service industries, product development is more tightly linked with market research on customer needs than with basic research and scientific developments. For instance, over the past several years, insurance companies have stepped up development of long-term-care insurance products, which pay for services ranging from home health assistants to nursing home care. They know that aging baby boomers will need to manage the expenses of that care, and the insurers need products they can sell profitably. This requires market research, experimentation, financial analysis, product design, and branding, all of which happens in product development units.

Scan and Search the Marketplace

Considering how easy it is to be blind-sided by competitors with new technologies, every company should systematically monitor its environment. Recall that the development that kills you probably won't come from a traditional competitor. Here are three hints for doing this correctly.

1. Identify what F. Michael Hruby calls "promontories," which are points that enable you to survey the competitive and technological landscape. These include magazines, technical journals, newsletters, conferences, and Web sites that cover your industry, customers' industries, and relevant products and technologies.

2. Pay attention to seemingly small developments that could conceivably affect you. Don't obsess about every little thing, but note things that could represent a threat if they were to grow. For instance, oil companies should be, and most likely are, monitoring hydrogen cell and bio-fuel technologies.

3. Watch anyone who sells products that are complementary to yours, and anyone who sells along the same value chain. For instance, could your suppliers become your competitors if they approached your customers with the right offering? Could they cut you out of the value chain? Barnes & Noble now publishes some books exclusively for its own stores. These are mainly repackaged classics now in the public domain, but it stills cuts publishers of those classics out of the value chain. Also, monitor merger and acquisition activity in your industry.

Promote Technology Transfer

Technology transfer is the way in which know-how moves from one arena to another. Generally it refers to movement from the laboratory to the marketplace, or from one economy to another. Scientific research generates discoveries and new technologies, and those technologies find their way into applications which, in the hands of specific companies, become products.

Scientists work on various research in university, corporate, and government laboratories around the world. They publish their findings (except for corporate trade secrets), and those findings fuel more research as well as technologies. Those technologies are applied to practical problems and then to products that can be sold to governments, businesses, and consumers. The Internet represents the best example of technology transfer over the past twenty-five years. The Internet is rooted in a telecommunications network developed by U.S. military researchers to enable government laboratories to communicate and, in a later network constructed by the National Science Foundation, to enable university labs to communicate with one another. In the mid-1990s, this network was made available to companies. Along the way, the merger of various networks and gateways and the development of standard communication protocols made the Internet more accessible.

However, until the development of the Web, only text messages could be sent over the Internet. The Web resulted from the development of hypertext markup language (HTML), which enabled the creation of Web pages and, along with communication protocols, browsers.

Reduce Time to Market

In 2006, a *BusinessWeek* survey found that "lengthy development times" were seen as the biggest barrier to innovation by major companies.

"Speed to market" has been the mantra of corporate innovators for several years. It may be hard to believe that lengthy development times can be a problem when consumers and businesses are swamped with new products, but that's the case.

To get the R & D and product development pipeline moving faster, companies:

- Create collaboration. Smart companies break down the walls between departments. They also create cross-functional teams.

- Open up. The concept of "open-sourcing" has caught on in many technology-driven businesses. For instance, Apple has been faulted for keeping its source code secret, which prevented independent developers from creating applications that would drive Apple's sales. In contrast, Microsoft promulgated its disk operating system (DOS) code and capitalized on the creativity of thousands of software developers.

- Use flexible production systems. The more flexibly manufacturing and service delivery systems can be configured, the more easily they can make and deliver new products and services.

- Improve intelligence. Many companies have become closer to their customers and suppliers to better understand their businesses and needs.

Speeding development cycles generates new products and compresses product life cycles. In a way, it's a self-sustaining treadmill on which companies must increase their speed to market because they have increased their speed to market. But whenever anything becomes a major point of competition, as quality did in the 1990s, companies raise the bar and improve their overall performance in that area. That's what has happened in innovation.

> **"** **INNOVATION** IS THE SPECIFIC TOOL OF ENTREPRENEURS, THE MEANS BY WHICH THEY **EXPLOIT CHANGE** AS AN OPPORTUNITY FOR A DIFFERENT BUSINESS OR A DIFFERENT SERVICE. **"**
>
> —Peter F. Drucker
> (author and
> management
> consultant)

The Innovative Entrepreneur

11

Innovators and entrepreneurs have two different, though overlapping, skill sets. Being an entrepreneur typically means dealing with employees or freelancers, suppliers, customers, media, and perhaps lenders and investors. An entrepreneur must make and sell a product and produce profits. These are pure business skills. Therefore, in this chapter I want to focus on those skills and the issues involved in starting a business based on an innovation.

Innovators and Entrepreneurs

An entrepreneur identifies, finances, and organizes the resources needed to start a business. Although the term "entrepreneur" applies to self-employed people in general, it is most properly applied to those associated with start-ups, which often center on innovations.

In my experience, innovators face five common problems on the way to becoming entrepreneurs:

1. Underestimating the work involved in running a business
2. Overspending or underspending on certain activities
3. Believing the product will sell itself
4. Mismanaging relationships
5. Failing to be disciplined and flexible

Let's look at each problem—and the relevant solution—individually.

Problem: Underestimating the Work Involved

It's no secret that starting and running a business is a lot of work. Yet many first-time entrepreneurs are still amazed by the amount of work it really takes. This occurs when they realize that they have to do everything.

Let's say you want to mail a sales letter and a CD-ROM demo to 300 people. Sounds simple, right? But you need current contact information on each person, in a spreadsheet or database file. Where does that info come from, and how does it get into the computer? You need business cards, letterhead, and envelopes. Who deals with the printer, approves the print job, and picks up the finished job? Who writes the sales letter, runs it off, signs it, and seals and stamps the envelopes? Who creates the content for the CD-ROMs, and then duplicates and packages them? The answers are you, your partner (if you have one), or someone you hire (if you can pay them).

Now, go through this kind of sequence for everything you need to do for the business. Everything has to be done by someone.

Solution: Plan Based on the Experience of Others

Define every goal and create a written plan for every goal. In that plan, define every task needed to complete each goal and every step needed to complete each task. Estimate the time needed by listening to people who have done it; then, if you're new at the task, add 20 to 50 percent, depending on the complexity. Be realistic about what you can do and what you can pay someone else to do.

Problem: Overspending or Underspending on Certain Activities

First, you must budget for every specific activity. If you say, "I'll need $80,000 to start this business and $7,500 a month to run it," that's not a budget. You must know the amount needed for every item and when you will need to spend it. Then you must follow the budget. The most common area where people overspend or underspend is in establishing their "business identity." Some go first-class with their offices, marketing materials, stationery, and Web site, and have little left for actual marketing (or paying themselves). Others do everything so cheaply that they appear unprofessional.

Solution: Skimp and Spend

Skimp on anything customers won't see. Buy secondhand furniture and file cabinets. Don't spend a lot to have a logo designed. (I used clip art from my printer's standard book.) Spend on efforts to reach and sell to customers. This rarely requires glossy full-color brochures. Instead, you need solid sales letters, a decent car and clothing, and a good Web site. Spend on travel and lodging to see prospects only after you've established that they're genuinely considering a purchase. Find a good freelance writer, graphic artist, and Web designer who will work at reasonable rates. Be very frank in discussing money with people. It's the essence of business.

Problem: Believing the Product Will Sell Itself

Seasoned entrepreneurs never make this mistake, but innovators often do. That's

Experiment with Marketing

Many novices believe that a certain marketing tool, such as advertising in a certain publication or mailing a news-letter or setting up a Web site, will automatically bring in business. It won't. Don't think that because the ad sales-person or Web site designer takes your order that you're making the right move. They get paid either way. Instead, do small experiments with direct mail, Web sites, direct selling, and public relations to see what works.

because innovators can become so enam-ored of their product that they believe everyone will be equally impressed and motivated. It doesn't work like that.

Solution: Sell Benefits and Value

Force yourself to think about what the prod-uct can do for your customers; whether they will save time, money, or other resources, or somehow make money or enjoy themselves. Those are the benefits and value. It takes disciplined thinking, as well as asking and listening, to identify the real value of your product or service to a customer.

Don't tell potential customers that your product slices onions quickly unless you know they love onions and they wish they could slice them faster.

Once you identify it, you must ascertain what your customer is most interested in, and how your product or service will deliver it to that prospect. Then you have to convey that value proposition to your prospect, and move them toward the sale.

Problem: Mismanaging Relationships

Many innovators who deal wonderfully with facts, ideas, issues, or things deal poorly with people. This gives rise to the stereotypes of the egghead inventor or the emotionally distant scientist. Most successful entrepreneurs have excellent people skills. Even if only on a business level, they understand human needs and motivation, and the give-and-take of relationships—and they act on that understanding. That means they can manage others, close sales, and resolve problems in ways that innovators who lack people skills cannot.

Solution: Acquire People Skills

Many innovators lack people skills, such as listening, empathizing, creating rapport, respecting others' views, compromising, and treating people as they want to be treated. If this describes you, then you must improve your people skills or partner with someone who has those skills. In the common "Mr. Inside, Mr. Outside" partnership, the innovator usually deals with the product and internal company matters, and the people person works with customers, investors, and other external parties.

Take Action
Visit www.nfte.com *to learn about the National Foundation for Teaching Entrepreneurship, which helps low-income young people become entrepreneurs.*

Problem: Failing to Be Disciplined and Flexible

Innovators often indulge in on-the-job intellectual stimulation (say, browsing the Web for hours) that entrepreneurs just can't fit in. Many innovators like to set their own hours, and check their e-mails and return phone calls when they get around to it. Yet customers expect people to be on the job during business hours and want prompt replies. Innovators also must learn the discipline of financial controls. Lack of flexibility can be a problem when business reversals occur. Belief in your innovation or business model is essential, but you can't let it blind you to a need to change. Some "believers" pile on the losses even after it's clear that things will never turn around.

Solution: Read Reality and Face Facts

True entrepreneurs remain rooted in realities. They work long and hard, but they also work smart. They exercise discipline and focus their efforts on the most important activities in the business—making sales, supporting customers, and dealing with finances. They monitor sales and expense figures at least weekly, watch market developments closely, and listen carefully. Thus, they operate in a businesslike way and either avoid problems or solve them quickly.

QUESTIONS A BUSINESS PLAN MUST ANSWER

- How large is the potential market for the product?

- Who are the founders and key employees?

- How will you make and sell the product?

- What are the potential sales and earnings?

The Business Plan

While every start-up will face problems, you can anticipate and prepare for them if you plan properly, which means writing a true business plan. Several good books, as well as Web sites, show how to write a business plan. It's an incredibly important document, and not just because investors and lenders want to see one before they give you money. Creating the plan forces you to understand the steps and tasks that will be necessary for the business to succeed, and to line up the resources needed to take those steps and complete those tasks.

Take Action

See Business Plans that Win $$$, *by Stanley Rich (Harper & Row, 1985), and the SBA's free online business planning course at* www.sba.gov/starting_business/index.html.

Think Big

If you have an innovation with real potential, you must think big. Microsoft, Apple, Amazon, FedEx, Dell, Starbucks, eBay, Google, and other major companies of recent vintage all started small, but then grew through solid planning and financing.

Almost every large company needed external financing at some point, usually in the early stages and during periods of expansion. That's because you have to spend money to develop, produce, and sell the product before you can generate sales and earnings.

Let's look at those outside sources of financing, especially for the start-up stage.

Finding Funding

Investors put money into a business to gain an ownership stake (known as equity) in it. They share in the earnings of the business, assuming there are any. In contrast, lenders put money into a business in return for interest payments on the loan, which must be repaid according to the terms of a loan agreement.

Investors and lenders in start-ups include:

○ *You and your family and friends*

○ *Wealthy individuals, known as "angels"*

○ *Small Business Administration*

○ *Venture capital firms*

○ *Large corporations, suppliers, and other sources*

One key to sound financing is to understand where the money to pay dividends to investors, or to repay a lender, will come from. Be sure you put any investors' or lenders' funds (or any funds, for that matter) into assets and activities that will generate money.

You, Your Family, and Friends

Entrepreneurs usually first use their savings and then personal bank loans and credit cards. Banks usually won't lend to a new venture unless the entrepreneurs have a track record. Banks extend personal loans based on the entrepreneur's personal creditworthiness.

Family members, relatives, and friends are typically the next stop. They should be treated like any other investor or lender you approach, and given the same information on the need for and uses of funds. Explain whether you are asking them to invest as owners or to lend you the money.

Wealthy Individuals

Certain wealthy individuals, or "angels," invest directly in new ventures, as opposed to investing through a venture capital fund. Angels tend to be savvy business-people with backgrounds in the kinds of businesses they consider backing.

You find angels through personal contacts and networking. They'll want to see a solid business plan and, if they invest enough, may want (and deserve) a seat on the company's board of directors or advisers. They often will have connections or advice that may contribute to your success.

Small Business Administration

The Small Business Administration (SBA) is an agency within the U.S. Department of Commerce that supports small businesses with information, training, and loan programs. The SBA would usually not be the best bet for a novice innovator. If you have a successful track record, though, definitely consider approaching the SBA. The agency is worth checking out for general information about starting a business as well as for other resources. For instance, SCORE (Service Corps of Retired Executives) is affiliated with the SBA, and its counselors offer guidance to small businesses of all types.

The SBA has too many loan programs to list here, so check out *www.sba.gov.*

Take Action
Check out www.circle lending.com *for information from Circle Lending about handling loans from family and friends.*

Venture Capital Firms

A venture capital firm (or VC) manages venture capital funds, which invest in companies from start-ups to rapidly growing outfits. Venture capital funds raise money mainly from individual and institutional investors.

Most venture capital firms receive a hundred business plans for every ten they consider, and invest in only one of those ten. Few invest in bread-and-butter businesses such as restaurants and retail stores, preferring technologies such as biotech, computers, software, and equipment for health care, aerospace, and other industries.

Venture capitalists generally require stock in the company, a seat on the board of directors, and a role in major decisions, which means that you give up some control when a venture fund invests in your business. Yet good venture capitalists contribute experience, contacts, and expertise that can help a company grow faster

> **in•i•tial pub•lic of•fer•ing (IPO)**
>
> 1. first offering of a corporation's stock to the investing public
> 2. mechanism by which early investors in the company receive their return

Take Action
You can find venture capital firms in the Directory of Venture Capital, *by Kate Lister and Tom Harnish (Wiley & Sons, 2000), on the World Wide Web, and by networking with other entrepreneurs.*

than it otherwise could. A venture capital firm also knows how to go about taking a company through its initial public offering (IPO).

Large Corporations

I discussed relations with large companies in Chapter 9, and would only emphasize that direct investment can be an alternative to a joint venture, licensing deal, or other corporate alliance. Suppliers rarely invest in a new company, but it does happen.

Raising the Stakes

Most start-ups are financed in stages. The founders work hard to make early sales and land significant customers, because the start-up must finance itself out of its sales. Many venture-backed companies take five years to be profitable; sophisticated investors and entrepreneurs understand that.

The Way of the Innovator

Whether you're an entrepreneur, a corporate manager or professional, or an individual operator, innovation gives you the thrill of novelty, the challenge of problem solving, and the reward of business success. Not everyone can be an innovator, but to the extent that you can, there is no more creative or exciting role to play in business.